EVERYTHING BABY
CROCHET

LEISURE ARTS, INC. • Maumelle, Arkansas

CONTENTS

Buttoned Sweater 5

Bear Bottle Cover 7

Beary Sweet Blanket 9

Baby Hat 12

Blanket 14

Wee Bib & Bottle Cover 16

Tunisian Cocoon & Cap 19

Rainbow Cube 27

Hat with Flower 32

Plaid Cocoon & Cap 35

Washcloth 39

Traditional Car Seat Cover 41

Ribbed Collar Sweater 43

Circles Blanket 46

Twinkle Twinkle Stroller Blanket ... 49

So Cute Safari Toy 53

Skirt Diaper Cover 59

Star Bright Toy 61

Pretzel Rattle 65

Irish Luck Blanket 66

Lexxi Dress 70

Puppy Lovie 73

Kitty Lovie 77

Lacy Cuff Boots 81

Kaleidoscope Throw 85

High-Top Sneakers 87

Double Dip Blanket 90

Giraffe Bib 93

Hat & Moccasins 95

Water Lilies Set 99

Ashley Dress 103

Fox Bib 105

Doll 109

Denim Diaper Cover 113

Cat Bottle Cover 115

Cables Car Seat Cover 119

Bubble Hat 121

Bobbling Away Blanket 125

Blue Blocks Blanket 128

Bluebell Ensemble 131

Instructions on pages 90-91.

BUTTONED SWEATER

 EASY

SIZE INFORMATION

Size	Finished Chest Measurement
6 months	21½" (54.5 cm)
12 months	23¾" (60.5 cm)
24 months	26" (66 cm)

Size Note: We have printed the instructions for the sizes in different colors to make it easier for you to find:
- Size 6 months in Blue
- Size 12 months in Pink
- Size 24 months in Green

Instructions in Black apply to all sizes.

GAUGE INFORMATION

14 sc and 16 rows = 4" (10 cm)

Gauge Swatch: 4" (10 cm) square
With Teal, ch 15.
Row 1: Sc in back ridge of second ch from hook *(Fig. 4, page 140)* and in each ch across: 14 sc.
Rows 2-16: Ch 1, turn; sc in each sc across.
Finish off.

STITCH GUIDE

SINGLE CROCHET 3 TOGETHER
(abbreviated sc3tog) (uses next 3 sts)
Pull up a loop in each of next 3 sts, YO and draw through all 4 loops on hook **(counts as one sc)**.

Work stripes as desired by changing colors at the ends of rows *(Fig. 7b, page 140)*.

BODY

With Teal, ch 130{142-154}.

Row 1: Working in back ridge of beginning ch *(Fig. 4, page 140)*, sc in second ch from hook and in next 28{30-32} chs, sc3tog, place split-ring marker in sc just made, sc in next 65{73-81} chs, sc3tog, place split-ring marker in sc just made, sc in last 29{31-33} chs: 125{137-149} sc.

SHOPPING LIST

Yarn
(Medium Weight) 4
[3.5 ounces, 200 yards (100 grams, 182 meters) per skein]:
☐ Teal - 1 skein
☐ Pink - 1 skein
☐ Rust - 1 skein
☐ Green - 1 skein
☐ White - 1 skein

Crochet Hook
☐ Size H (5 mm)
  or size needed for gauge

Additional Supplies
☐ Split-ring stitch markers - 2
☐ Safety pin
☐ Yarn needle
☐ Sewing needle and thread
☐ ½" (12 mm) Buttons - 3

BUTTONED SWEATER

Row 2 (Right side): Ch 1, turn; ★ sc in each sc across to within one sc of marked sc, sc3tog, move marker to sc just made; repeat from ★ once **more**, sc in each sc across: 121{133-145} sc.

Note: Loop a short piece of yarn around any stitch to mark Row 2 as **right** side.

Rows 3 thru 16{18-20}: Ch 1, turn; ★ sc in each sc across to within one sc of marked sc, sc3tog, move marker to sc just made; repeat from ★ once **more**, sc in each sc across: 65{69-73} sc.

Row 17{19-21}: Ch 1, turn; ★ sc in each st across to marked sc, 3 sc in marked sc, remove marker; repeat from ★ once **more**, sc in each sc across: 69{73-77} sc.

Rows 18{20-22} thru 30{34-36}: Ch 1, turn; ★ sc in each sc across to center sc of next 3-sc group, 3 sc in center sc; repeat from ★ once **more**, sc in each sc across: 121{133-137} sc.

Finish off.

Neck Shaping

Row 1: With **wrong** side facing, skip first 6{7-8} sc and join Teal with sc in next sc *(see Joining With Sc, page 138)*; ★ sc in each sc across to center sc of next 3-sc group, 3 sc in center sc; repeat from ★ once **more**, sc in each sc across to last 6{7-8} sc, leave last 6{7-8} sc unworked: 113{123-125} sc.

Rows 2 thru 4{6-8}: Ch 1, turn; ★ sc in each sc across to center sc of next 3-sc group, 3 sc in center sc; repeat from ★ once **more**, sc in each sc across: 125{143-153} sc.

Buttonhole Row - Girls Only: Ch 1, turn; sc in first sc, (ch 1, skip next sc, sc in next 5 sc) twice, ch 1, skip next sc, ★ sc in each sc across to center sc of next 3-sc group, 3 sc in center sc; repeat from ★ once **more**, sc in each sc across: 126{144-154} sc and 3 ch-1 sps.

Buttonhole Row - Boys Only: Ch 1, turn; ★ sc in each sc across to center sc of next 3-sc group, 3 sc in center sc; repeat from ★ once **more**, sc in each sc across to last 14 sc, ch 1, skip next sc, (sc in next 5 sc, ch 1, skip next sc) twice, sc in last sc: 126{144-154} sc and 3 ch-1 sps.

Last Row: Ch 1, turn; sc in each sc and in each ch-1 sp across working 3 sc in center sc of each 3-sc group; do not finish off: 133{151-161} sc.

Place loop from hook on safety pin so piece will not unravel as you are sewing the shoulder/sleeve seams. With **wrong** side facing and Teal, sew each shoulder/sleeve seam from last row of Body to wrist *(see How to Fold & Sew, page 144)*.

Edging

Slip loop from safety pin onto hook; with **right** side facing, ch 1; 2 sc in first sc, sc in end of each row across Neck Shaping and in each unworked sc of last row on Body; working in free loops of beginning ch *(Fig. 6b, page 140)*, sc in each ch across; sc in each unworked sc of last row on Body and in end of each row across Neck Shaping to last row, 3 sc in last row, sc in each sc around working 3 sc in center sc of each 3-sc group, sc in same st as first sc; join with slip st to first sc, finish off.

Sew buttons to front opposite buttonholes.

Design by Darla Sims.

BEAR BOTTLE COVER

 EASY

Finished Size: Fits an 8 ounce bottle

GAUGE INFORMATION
Gauge Swatch: 2" (5 cm) diameter
With larger size hook, work same as Cover for 4 rnds: 24 sc.

STITCH GUIDE
TREBLE CROCHET *(abbreviated tr)*
YO twice, insert hook in st indicated, YO and pull up a loop (4 loops on hook), (YO and draw through 2 loops on hook) 3 times.

COVER
With larger size hook and Brown, ch 4; join with slip st to form a ring.

Rnd 1 (Right side): 2 Sc in same st and in each ch around; do **not** join, place marker to indicated beginning of rnd *(see Marker, page 140)*: 8 sc.

Rnd 2: 2 Sc in each sc around: 16 sc.

Rnd 3: (Sc in next sc, 2 sc in next sc) around: 24 sc.

Rnds 4-14: Sc in each sc around.

Rnd 15: (Ch 1, sc in next sc) around.

Rnd 16: (Skip next ch-1 sp, sc in next sc) around.

Rnds 17-25: Repeat Rnds 15 and 16, 4 times; then repeat Rnd 15 once **more**.

Finish off.

HEAD
With smaller size hook and Brown, ch 4; join with slip st to form a ring.

Rnd 1: 2 Sc in same st and in each ch around; do **not** join, place marker: 8 sc.

Rnd 2: (Sc in next sc, 2 sc in next sc) around: 12 sc.

Rnd 3: Sc in each sc around.

Rnd 4: Sc in next 5 sc, 5 sc in next sc, sc in each sc around: 16 sc.

Rnd 5: Sc in each sc around.

Rnd 6: (Sc in next sc, 2 sc in next sc) around: 24 sc.

Rnds 7 and 8: Sc in each sc around.

Rnd 9 (Ears): Sc in next 7 sc, † work (slip st, hdc, 5 dc, hdc, slip st) in Front Loops Only of next sc *(Fig. 5, page 140)* †, sc in **both** loops of next 5 sc, repeat from † to † once, sc in **both** loops of each sc around.

SHOPPING LIST

Yarn
(Medium Weight)
☐ Brown - 85 yards
 (77.5 meters)
☐ Black - small amount

Crochet Hook
☐ Size F (3.75 mm) **and**
☐ Size G (4 mm)
  or sizes needed for gauge

Additional Supplies
☐ Polyester stuffing
☐ ½" Ribbon - 15" (43 cm)
☐ Yarn needle

BEAR BOTTLE COVER

Rnd 10: Sc in next 7 sc, sc in free loops of next sc **behind** Ear *(Fig. 6a, page 140)*, sc in **both** loops of next 5 sc, sc in free loops of next sc **behind** Ear, sc in **both** loops of each sc around.

Rnd 11: (Skip next sc, sc in next 2 sc) around: 16 sc.

Stuff Head lightly with polyester fiberfill.

Rnd 12: (Skip next sc, sc in next sc) around: 8 sc.

Rnd 13: (Skip next sc, slip st in next sc) around; finish off leaving a long end for sewing.

ARM (Make 2)

With smaller size hook and Brown, ch 4; join with slip st to form a ring.

Rnd 1 (Right side): 2 Sc in same st and in each ch around; do **not** join, place marker: 8 sc.

Rnd 2: (Sc in next sc, 2 sc in next sc) around: 12 sc.

Rnd 3: Sc in each sc around.

Rnd 4: (Skip next sc, sc in next 2 sc) around: 8 sc.

Rnds 5-9: Sc in each sc around.

Rnd 10: (Skip next sc, slip st in next sc) around; finish off leaving a long end for sewing.
Flatten Arm.

LEG (Make 2)

With smaller size hook and Brown, ch 4; join with slip st to form a ring.

Rnd 1: 2 Sc in same st and in each ch around; do **not** join, place marker: 8 sc.

Rnd 2: (Sc in next sc, 2 sc in next sc) around: 12 sc.

Rnds 3 and 4: Sc in each sc around.

Stuff Leg lightly with polyester fiberfill.

Rnd 5: (Skip next sc, sc in next 2 sc) around: 8 sc.

Rnds 6-10: Sc in each sc around.

Rnd 11: (Skip next sc, slip st in next sc) around; finish off leaving a long end for sewing.

FINISHING

Using photo as a guide for placement:
Sew Arms and Legs to Cover.

Using Embroidery Stitches on page 143, add facial features to Head and accent lines to Legs.

Tie ribbon in a bow around neck.

Design by Sue Penrod.

BERRY SWEET BLANKET

 EASY

Finished Size: 34½" x 49½" (87.5 cm x 125.5 cm)

GAUGE INFORMATION
17 sts = 4" (10 cm)
   Each Square = 7½" (19 cm)
Gauge Swatch: 2¾" (7 cm) square
Work same as Square through Rnd 3: 36 dc and 12 ch-1 sps.

STITCH GUIDE
TREBLE CROCHET *(abbreviated tr)*
YO twice, insert hook in sc indicated, YO and pull up a loop (4 loops on hook), (YO and draw through 2 loops on hook) 3 times.

FRONT POST TREBLE CROCHET
   (abbreviated FPtr)
YO twice, insert hook from **front** to **back** around post of st indicated *(Fig. 10, page 141)*, YO and pull up a loop (4 loops on hook), (YO and draw through 2 loops on hook) 3 times.

FRONT POST DOUBLE TREBLE CROCHET
   (abbreviated FPdtr)
YO 3 times, insert hook from **front** to **back** around post of st indicated *(Fig. 10, page 141)*, YO and pull up a loop (5 loops on hook), (YO and draw through 2 loops on hook) 4 times.

SQUARE (Make 24)
With Hot Pink, ch 4; join with slip st to form a ring.

Rnd 1 (Right side)**:** Ch 3 (**counts as first dc, now and throughout**), 2 dc in ring, ch 1, (3 dc in ring, ch 1) 3 times; join with slip st to first dc, finish off: 12 dc and 4 ch-1 sps.

Note: Loop a short piece of yarn around any stitch to mark Rnd 1 as **right** side.

Rnd 2: With **right** side facing, join Pink with dc in any ch-1 sp *(see Joining With Dc, page 139)*; (2 dc, ch 1, 3 dc) in same sp, skip next 3 dc, ★ (3 dc, ch 1, 3 dc) in next ch-1 sp, skip next 3 dc; repeat from ★ 2 times **more**; join with slip st to first dc, finish off: 24 dc and 4 ch-1 sps.

Rnd 3: With **right** side facing, join White with dc in any ch-1 sp; (2 dc, ch 1, 3 dc) in same sp, ch 1, skip next 3 dc, 3 dc in sp **before** next dc *(Fig. 8, page 141)*, ch 1, skip next 3 dc, ★ (3 dc, ch 1) twice in next ch-1 sp, skip next 3 dc, 3 dc in sp before next dc, ch 1, skip next 3 dc; repeat from ★ 2 times **more**; join with slip st to first dc, finish off: 36 dc and 12 ch-1 sps.

SHOPPING LIST

Yarn
(Medium Weight) [4]
[3½ ounces, 170 yards
(100 grams, 156 meters)
   per skein]:
☐ Pink - 5 skeins
☐ Hot Pink - 4 skeins
☐ White - 3 skeins

Crochet Hook
☐ Size F (3.75 mm)
   or size needed for gauge

Additional Supplies
☐ Yarn needle

Berry Sweet Blanket

Rnd 4: With **right** side facing, join Hot Pink with dc in any corner ch-1 sp; ★ † work FPdtr around third dc of 3-dc group one rnd below **(before corner ch)**, (dc, ch 1, dc) in same corner sp as last dc made, work FPdtr around first dc of next 3-dc group one rnd **below (after corner ch)**, dc in same corner sp as last dc made, ch 1, (3 dc in next ch-1 sp, ch 1) twice †, dc in next corner ch-1 sp; repeat from ★ 2 times **more**, then repeat from † to † once; join with slip st to first dc, finish off: 48 sts and 16 ch-1 sps.

Rnd 5: With **right** side facing, join Pink with dc in any corner ch-1 sp; (2 dc, ch 1, 3 dc) in same sp, ch 1, working in sts and in chs, skip next 2 sts, dc in next 3 sts, ch 1, (skip next dc, dc in next 3 sts, ch 1) twice, skip next 2 sts, ★ (3 dc, ch 1) twice in next corner ch-1 sp, working in sts and in chs, skip next 2 sts, dc in next 3 sts, ch 1, (skip next dc, dc in next 3 sts, ch 1) twice, skip next 2 sts; repeat from ★ 2 times **more**; join with slip st to first dc, finish off: 60 dc and 20 ch-1 sps.

Rnd 6: With **right** side facing, join Hot Pink with dc in any corner ch-1 sp; ★ † work FPdtr around FPdtr one rnd below, (dc, ch 1, dc) in same corner sp as last dc made, work FPdtr around FPdtr one rnd below, dc in same corner sp as last dc made, ch 1, (3 dc in next ch-1 sp, ch 1) 4 times †, dc in next corner ch-1 sp; repeat from ★ 2 times **more**, then repeat from † to † once; join with slip st to first dc, finish off: 72 sts and 24 ch-1 sps.

Rnd 7: With **right** side facing, join Pink with dc in any corner ch-1 sp; (2 dc, ch 1, 3 dc) in same sp, ch 1, ★ † 3 dc in next ch-1 sp, [work FPtr around first dc of 3-dc group one rnd below next ch-1 sp, dc in ch-1 sp, work FPtr around third dc of same 3-dc group one rnd below, skip next dc, dc in next dc] 3 times, 2 dc in next ch-1 sp, ch 1 †, (3 dc, ch 1) twice in next corner ch-1 sp; repeat from ★ 2 times **more**, then repeat from † to † once; join with slip st to first dc, finish off: 92 sts and 12 ch-1 sps.

Rnd 8: With **right** side facing, join Hot Pink with dc in any corner ch-1 sp; (2 dc, ch 1, 3 dc) in same sp, ch 1, ★ † dc in next ch-1 sp, work FPtr around FPdtr one rnd below, dc in same sp as last dc made, ch 1, skip next 3 dc, dc in next 11 sts, ch 1, dc in next ch-1 sp, work FPtr around FPdtr one rnd below, dc in same sp as last dc made, ch 1 †, (3 dc, ch 1) twice in next corner ch-1 sp; repeat from ★ 2 times **more**, then repeat from † to † once; join with slip st to first dc, finish off: 92 sts and 20 ch-1 sps.

Rnd 9: With **right** side facing, join White with dc in any corner ch-1 sp; ch 1, 3 dc in same sp, ch 1, ★ † (3 dc in next ch-1 sp, ch 1) twice, skip next 3 dc, (3 dc in next dc, ch 1, skip next 3 dc) twice, (3 dc in next ch-1 sp, ch 1) twice †, (3 dc, ch 1) twice in next corner ch-1 sp; repeat from ★ 2 times **more**, then repeat from † to † once, 2 dc in same sp as first dc; join with slip st to first dc, finish off leaving a long end for sewing: 96 dc and 32 ch-1 sps.

ASSEMBLY

Thread yarn needle with long end. With **wrong** sides together and working through **both** loops on **both** pieces, whipstitch 2 Squares together *(Fig. 13a, page 142)*.

Join remaining Squares forming 4 vertical strips of 6 Squares each; then join strips together in same manner.

TRIM

Rnd 1: With **right** side facing, join White with dc in any corner ch-1 sp; (2 dc, ch 1, 3 dc) in same sp, ch 1, ★ † (3 dc in next ch-1 sp, ch 1) 7 times, [3 dc in next joining, ch 1, (3 dc in next ch-1 sp, ch 1) 7 times] across to next corner ch-1 sp †, (3 dc, ch 1) twice in corner ch-1 sp; repeat from ★ 2 times **more**, then repeat from † to † once; join with slip st to first dc, finish off: 492 dc and 164 ch-1 sps.

First Side

Row 1: With **wrong** side facing and working across long edge, join Pink with sc in first corner ch-1 sp *(see Joining With Sc, page 138)*; sc in next 3 dc, sc in next ch-1 sp and in next 3 dc, ★ skip next ch-1 sp, sc in next 3 dc, (sc in next ch-1 sp and in next 3 dc) 3 times; repeat from ★ across to within 3 ch-1 sps of next corner ch-1 sp, skip next ch-1 sp, (sc in next 3 dc and in next ch-1 sp) 3 times: 185 sc.

Row 2: Ch 1, turn; sc in each st across.

Row 3: Ch 1, turn; sc in first sc, (tr in next sc, sc in next sc pushing tr to right side) across.

Rows 4-8: Repeat Rows 2 and 3 twice, then repeat Row 2 once **more**; at end of Row 8, finish off.

Second Side

Working across opposite long edge, work same as First Side.

First End

Row 1: With **wrong** side facing and working across short edge, join Pink with sc in end of first row on First Side; work 6 sc evenly spaced across end of rows; sc in sp on next Square and in next 3 dc, sc in next ch-1 sp and in next 3 dc, ★ skip next ch-1 sp, sc in next 3 dc, (sc in next ch-1 sp and in next 3 dc) 3 times; repeat from ★ 6 times **more**, skip next ch-1 sp, (sc in next 3 dc and in next ch-1 sp) 3 times; work 7 sc evenly spaced across end of rows on Second Side: 139 sc.

Rows 2-8: Work same as First Side.

Second End

Working across opposite short edge, work same as First End.

Design by Carol Holding.

BABY HAT

 EASY

SIZE INFORMATION
Finished Sizes:
Infant: 14¼" (36 cm) circumference
Toddler: 16½" (42 cm) circumference

Size Note: We have printed the instructions for the sizes in different colors to make it easier for you to find:
· Infant in Blue
· Child in Pink
Instructions in Black apply to both sizes.

GAUGE INFORMATION
In Ribbing, with larger size hook,
 12 sts = 3¼" (8.25 cm),
 8 rows = 3" (7.5 cm)
Note: Row gauge for the Ribbing is very important since it determines the finished circumference.
In Body pattern, with smaller size hook, 9 sts = 2½" (6.25 cm)
Gauge Swatch: 3¼" wide x 3" high
 (8.25 cm x 7.5 cm)
With Cream, ch 13.
Work same as Ribbing Rows 1-8: 12 sts. For Infant Size, if your gauge is the correct size, you can continue to work Ribbing; for Toddler Size, finish off.

STITCH GUIDE
FRONT POST DOUBLE CROCHET
 (abbreviated FPdc)
YO, insert hook from **front** to **back** around post of dc indicated, YO and pull up a loop (3 loops on hook), (YO and draw through 2 loops on hook) twice *(Fig. 10, page 141)*.

RIBBING
The Ribbing is worked to the circumference of the hat and will be folded in half lengthwise to form a brim.

Using larger size hook and Cream, ch 13{17}; place a marker in first ch from hook to make it easier to find at the end of Row 2.

Row 1: Hdc in third ch from hook **(2 skipped chs count as first hdc)** and in each ch across: 12{16} hdc.

Row 2: Ch 1, turn; sc in Back Loop Only of each hdc across *(Fig. 5, page 140)* including marked st; remove marker.

Row 3: Ch 2 **(counts as first hdc)**, turn; hdc in Back Loop Only of next sc and each sc across.

SHOPPING LIST

Yarn
(Medium Weight)
[6 ounces, 315 yards (170 grams, 288 meters) per skein]:
☐ Cream - 1 skein
☐ Black - 1 skein

Crochet Hooks
☐ Size G (4 mm) **and**
☐ Size I (5.5 mm)
 or sizes needed for gauge

Additional Supplies
☐ Yarn needle
☐ Removable markers or scrap yarn

Rows 4 thru 38{44}: Repeat Rows 2 and 3, 17{20} times; then repeat Row 2 once **more**.

BODY

Change to smaller size hook.

Row 1: Ch 1, working across end of rows, sc in first sc row, 2 sc in next hdc row, (sc in next sc row, 2 sc in next hdc row) across: 57{66} sc.

Row 2: Ch 3 (**counts as first dc**), turn; dc in next sc and in each sc across to last sc, dc in last sc changing to Black (*Fig. 7d, page 140*).

Carry the unused yarn up the side. The carried strands will be hidden when sewing the seam.

Row 3 (Right side)**:** Ch 1, turn; sc in first dc, work FPdc around next dc, ★ sc in next 2 dc, work FPdc around next dc; repeat from ★ across to last dc, sc in last dc: 19{22} FPdc and 38{44} sc.

Row 4: Ch 3, turn; dc in next st and in each st across to last sc, dc in last sc changing to Cream: 57{66} dc.

Row 5: Ch 1, turn; sc in first dc, work FPdc around FPdc in row below next dc, skip dc behind FPdc just made, ★ sc in next 2 dc, work FPdc around FPdc in row below next dc, skip dc behind FPdc just made; repeat from ★ across to last dc, sc in last dc: 19{22} FPdc and 38{44} sc.

Row 6: Ch 3, turn; dc in next st and in each st across to last sc, dc in last sc changing to next color: 57{66} dc.

Rows 7 thru 16{20}: Repeat Rows 5 and 6, 5{7} times.

Cut Cream leaving a long end for sewing. Finish off Black.

Fold the Body in half with **right** side together, matching end of rows. Using Cream, whipstitch (*Figs. 13a & 13c, page 142*) across Body making sure that the carried strands don't show on the right side, then whipstitch across Ribbing. Fold the Ribbing in half to the **wrong** side matching the bottom edge to Row 1 of the Body; sew in place.

Flatten the Hat with **wrong** side together and the seam centered at the back. Using Cream, whipstitch top seam allowing the stitching to show.

POM-POM (Make 2)

Make 3" (7.5 cm) pom-pom using black and white (*Figs. 16a-c, page 143*).

Attach one pom-pom to each corner of the Body, pull the ends to the **wrong** side a few stitches apart and tie the ends together; secure in place.

Design by Sharon H. Silverman.

BLANKET

EASY

SIZE INFORMATION

Car Seat Blanket: 29" x 35"
  (73.5 cm x 89 cm)
Doll Blanket: 29" x 35"
  (73.5 cm x 89 cm)

GAUGE INFORMATION

In pattern, 10 sts = 3" (7.5 cm)
Gauge Swatch: 3" (7.5 cm) wide
With Color A, ch 11.
Row 1: Hdc in second ch from hook and in each ch across: 10 hdc.
Rows 2-6: Ch 1, turn; hdc in each hdc across.
Finish off.

STITCH GUIDE

BEGINNING LINKED DOUBLE CROCHET
(abbreviated beginning linked dc)
Insert hook in second ch from hook, YO and pull up a loop, insert hook in first hdc, YO and pull up a loop (3 loops on hook), (YO and draw through 2 loops on hook) twice.

LINKED DOUBLE CROCHET
(abbreviated linked dc)
Insert hook in horizontal bar of previous linked dc *(Fig. A)*, YO and pull up a loop, insert hook in next st, YO and pull up a loop (3 loops on hook) *(Fig. B)*, (YO and draw through 2 loops on hook) twice *(Fig. C)*.

SHOPPING LIST

Yarn
(Medium Weight) 4
[6 ounces, 315 yards (170.1 grams, 288 meters) per skein]:
☐ Color A (Pink) - 1 skein
☐ Color B (Grey) - 1 skein
☐ Color C (White) - 1 skein

Note: Light weight yarn can be used when needed to match the color of the toy as long as gauge can be cheived.

Crochet Hook
☐ Size 7 (4.5 mm)
  or size needed for gauge

Additional Supplies
☐ Yarn needle

Fig. A
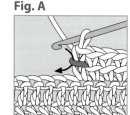

Fig. B
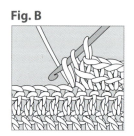

Fig. C
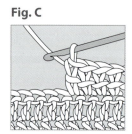

14 www.leisurearts.com

BODY

With Color B, ch 96{39}.

Row 1 (Right side): Hdc in second ch from hook and in each ch across changing to Color C in last hdc *(Fig. 7c, page 140)*: 95{38} hdc.

Row 2: Ch 1, turn; hdc in each hdc across changing to Color A in last hdc.

Row 3: Ch 2 (**does not count as a st**), turn; dc in each hdc across changing to Color B in last dc *(Fig. 7d, page 140)*.

Row 4: Ch 1, turn; hdc in each dc across changing to Color C in last hdc.

Repeat Rows 2-4 for pattern until Body measures approximately 34½{11½}"/87.5{29} cm from beginning ch, ending by working Row 2.

EDGING

With Color A, ch 2, turn; work beginning linked dc, work linked dc around entire edge, working 4 linked dc in each corner; join with slip st to first st, finish off.

Design by Tamara Ramsey.

WEE BIB & BOTTLE COVER

 **EASY**

Finished Bib Size: 8¼" x 9½" (21 cm x 24 cm)
Finished Bottle Cover Size: Fits an 8 ounce bottle

GAUGE INFORMATION
17 sc and 19 rows = 4" (10 cm)
Gauge Swatch: 4" (10 cm) square
With White, ch 18.
Row 1: Sc in second ch from hook and in each ch across: 17 sc.
Rows 2-19: Ch 1, turn; sc in each sc across.
Finish off.

STITCH GUIDE
SINGLE CROCHET 2 TOGETHER
   (abbreviated sc2tog)
Pull up a loop in each of next 2 sc, YO and draw through all 3 loops on hook **(counts as one sc)**.
BEGINNING POPCORN (uses one st)
Ch 3 **(counts as first dc, now and throughout)**, 2 dc in st indicated, drop loop from hook, insert hook in first dc of 3-dc group, hook dropped loop and draw through st.
POPCORN (uses one sc)
3 dc in sc indicated, drop loop from hook, insert hook in first dc of 3-dc group, hook dropped loop and draw through st.

BIB
Body
With White, ch 3.

Row 1: Sc in second ch from hook and in last ch: 2 sc.

Row 2 (Right side): Ch 1, turn; 2 sc in each sc across: 4 sc.

Note: Loop a short piece of yarn around any stitch to mark Row 2 as **right** side.

Rows 3-15: Ch 1, turn; 2 sc in first sc, sc in each sc across to last sc, 2 sc in last sc: 30 sc.

Rows 16-20: Ch 1, turn; sc in each sc across.

Rows 21-23: Ch 1, turn; beginning in first sc, sc2tog, sc in each sc across to last 2 sc, sc2tog: 24 sc.

Rows 24-31: Ch 1, turn; sc in each sc across.

SHOPPING LIST

Yarn
(Medium Weight)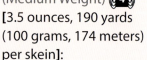
[3.5 ounces, 190 yards (100 grams, 174 meters) per skein]:
☐ Pink - 1 skein
☐ White - 1 skein

Crochet Hook
☐ Size F (3.75 mm)
   or size needed for gauge

Additional Supplies
Ribbon:
☐ ¼" (7 mm) wide - 12" (30.5 cm) for Bib
☐ ⅛" (3 mm) wide - 12" (30.5 cm) for Bottle Cover

Row 32: Ch 1, turn; beginning in first sc, sc2tog, sc in each sc across to last 2 sc, sc2tog; do **not** finish off: 22 sc.

RIGHT SIDE

Row 1: Ch 1, turn; sc in first 7 sc, leave remaining 15 sc unworked: 7 sc.

Row 2 (Decrease row)**:** Ch 1, turn; beginning in first sc, sc2tog, sc in each sc across: 6 sc.

Row 3 (Decrease row)**:** Ch 1, turn; sc in each sc across to last 2 sc, sc2tog: 5 sc.

Rows 4 and 5: Repeat Rows 2 and 3: 3 sc.

Row 6: Ch 1, turn; beginning in first sc, sc2tog, sc in last sc; finish off: 2 sc.

LEFT SIDE

Row 1: With **wrong** side facing, skip next 8 sc from Right Side on Row 32 of Body and join White with sc in next sc *(see Joining With Sc, page 138)*; sc in each sc across: 7 sc.

Row 2 (Decrease row)**:** Ch 1, turn; sc in each sc across to last 2 sc, sc2tog: 6 sc.

Row 3 (Decrease row)**:** Ch 1, turn; beginning in first sc, sc2tog, sc in each sc across: 5 sc.

Rows 4 and 5: Repeat Rows 2 and 3: 3 sc.

Row 6: Ch 1, turn; sc in first sc, sc2tog; finish off: 2 sc.

Edging

With **right** side facing, join Pink with sc in first sc on Row 6 of Right Side; sc in same st, 2 sc in next sc; work 40 sc evenly spaced across end of rows; working in free loops of beginning ch *(Fig. 6b, page 140)*, 2 sc in ch at base of first sc and in last ch; work 39 sc evenly spaced across end of rows; sc in first sc on Row 6 of Left Side, place marker around sc just made for Left Tie placement, sc in same st, 2 sc in last sc; sc in end of first 6 rows; sc in next 8 skipped sc on Body; sc in end of first 6 rows on Right Side; join with slip st to first sc, do not finish off: 111 sc.

RIGHT TIE

Row 1: Ch 1, do **not** turn; beginning in same st, sc2tog twice, leave remaining sc unworked: 2 sc.

Row 2: Ch 1, turn; beginning in first sc, sc2tog, chain a 12" (30.5 cm) length; finish off.

LEFT TIE

Row 1: With **right** side facing, join Pink with slip st in marked sc on Left Side; ch 1, beginning in same st, sc2tog twice, leave remaining sc unworked: 2 sc.

Row 2: Ch 1, turn; beginning in first st, sc2tog, chain a 12" (30.5 cm) length; finish off.

Trim

With **right** side facing, join Pink with slip st in end of Row 1 on Right Tie; working in sc on Edging, skip first sc, 3 dc in next sc, skip next sc, ★ sc in next sc, skip next sc, 3 dc in next sc, skip next sc; repeat from ★ around to Left Tie, slip st in end of Row 1 on Left Tie, finish off.

Using photo as a guide for placement, tie ribbon in a bow; then sew bow to Bib.

BOTTLE COVER
Bottom

Rnd 1 (Right side): With Pink, ch 2, 6 sc in second ch from hook; join with slip st to first sc.

Note: Mark Rnd 1 as **right** side.

Rnd 2: Ch 1, 2 sc in same st as joining and in each sc around; join with slip st to first sc: 12 sc.

Rnd 3: Ch 1, sc in same st as joining, 2 sc in next sc, (sc in next sc, 2 sc in next sc) around; join with slip st to first sc: 18 sc.

Rnd 4: Ch 1, sc in same st as joining and in next sc, 2 sc in next sc, (sc in next 2 sc, 2 sc in next sc) around; join with slip st to Back Loop Only of first sc *(Fig. 5, page 140)*, do **not** finish off: 24 sc.

Sides

Rnd 1: Ch 1, working in Back Loops Only, 2 sc in same st as joining, sc in next 5 sc, (2 sc in next sc, sc in next 5 sc) around; join with slip st to both loops of first sc: 28 sc.

Rnd 2: Ch 1, sc in both loops of same st as joining and each sc around; join with slip st to first sc.

Rnd 3: Ch 1, sc in same st as joining, skip next sc, 3 dc in next sc, skip next sc, ★ sc in next sc, skip next sc, 3 dc in next sc, skip next sc; repeat from ★ around; join with slip st to first sc: 7 sc and 21 dc.

Rnds 4 and 5: Slip st in next 2 dc, ch 1, sc in same st, 3 dc in next sc, skip next dc, ★ sc in next dc, 3 dc in next sc, skip next st; repeat from ★ around; at end of Rnd 5 change to White in last dc *(Fig. 7d, page 140)*; join with slip st to first sc.

Rnds 6-11: Ch 1, sc in same st as joining and in each st around; join with slip st to first sc; at end of Rnd 11 change to Pink in last sc: 28 sc.

Rnds 12-20: Repeat Rnds 3-11.

Rnd 21 (Eyelet rnd): Ch 1, sc in same st as joining, ch 1, skip next sc, ★ sc in next sc, ch 1, skip next sc; repeat from ★ around; join with slip st to first sc: 14 ch-1 sps.

Rnd 22: Slip st in first ch-1 sp, ch 1, sc in same sp, (ch 3, sc in next ch-1 sp) around, ch 1, hdc in first sc to form last ch-3 sp: 14 ch-3 sps.

Rnd 23: Ch 1, sc in last ch-3 sp made, ch 3, (sc in next ch-3 sp, ch 3) around; join with slip st to first sc, finish off.

Weave ribbon through ch-1 sps on Eyelet round; tie ends in a bow.

Design by Jan Hatfield.

TUNISIAN COCOON & CAP

# TUNISIAN COCOON & CAP

EASY

Finished Size Cocoon: 25" long x 26" circumference (63.5 x 66 cm)
Cap: Fits Newborn to 3 months

We recommend working the gauge swatch to learn the technique of working Tunisian Stitch in the round with a double ended crochet hook. We used Blue for the first ball of yarn and Tan for the second ball of yarn for our sample.

GAUGE INFORMATION

In pattern, 14 sts and 14 rnds = 4" (10 cm)

Gauge Swatch: 4" long x 8½" circumference (10 x 21.5 cm)

With Blue and using double ended hook, ch 30; being careful **not** to twist ch, join with slip st to form a ring, place marker in loop on hook to mark beginning of rnd and **right** side *(Fig. A, page 21)*. Marked loop counts as first vertical bar.

Rnd 1
Step A: Working in back ridge of beginning ch *(Fig. 4, page 140)*, (Insert hook in next ch, YO and pull up a loop) 14 times, leave remaining 15 chs unworked *(Fig. B, page 21)*: 15 loops on hook.

Step B: Drop Blue, turn work around; slide loops to opposite end of hook *(Fig. C, page 21)*; with Tan, [YO and draw through 2 loops on hook *(Figs. D & E, page 21)*] across until 2 loops remain on hook.

Step C: Drop Tan, turn work around; slide last 2 loops to opposite end of hook; with Blue and working in back ridge of beginning ch, (insert hook in next ch, YO and pull up a loop) 15 times: 17 loops on hook.

Step D: Drop Blue, turn work around; slide loops to opposite end of hook; with Tan, (YO and draw through 2 loops on hook) across until 2 loops remain on hook.

Rnd 2
Step A: Drop Tan, turn work around; slide last 2 loops to opposite end of hook, insert hook under marked vertical bar *(Fig. F, page 21)*; with Blue, YO and pull up a loop, move marker to loop just made *(Fig. G, page 21)*, (insert hook under next vertical bar, YO and pull up a loop) 14 times: 17 loops on hook.

SHOPPING LIST

Yarn
(Medium Weight) [4]
[4 ounces, 204 yards (113 grams, 187 meters) per skein]:
☐ Variegated - 3 skeins
[5 ounces, 256 yards (142 grams, 234 meters) per skein]:
☐ Blue - 1 skein

Double Ended Tunisian Hook
☐ Size K (6.5 mm)
 or size needed for gauge

Standard Crochet Hook
☐ Size K (6.5 mm)

Additional Supplies
☐ Split-ring marker
☐ Yarn needle

Step B: Drop Blue, turn work around; slide loops to opposite end of hook; with Tan, (YO and draw through 2 loops on hook) across until 2 loops remain on hook.

Step C: Drop Tan, turn work around; slide last 2 loops to opposite end of hook; with Blue, (insert hook under next vertical bar, YO and pull up a loop) 15 times: 17 loops on hook.

Step D: Drop Blue, turn work around; slide loops to opposite end of hook; with Tan, (YO and draw through 2 loops on hook) across until 2 loops remain on hook: 30 vertical bars.

Rnds 3-14: Repeat Rnd 2, 12 times; at end of Rnd 14, with Tan, YO and draw through last 2 loops; finish off, cut Blue.

STITCH GUIDE

BACK POST DOUBLE CROCHET

(abbreviated BPdc)

YO, insert hook from **back** to **front** around post of st indicated *(Fig. 10, page 141)*, YO and pull up a loop (3 loops on hook), (YO and draw through 2 loops on hook) twice. Skip st in **front** of BPdc.

FRONT POST DOUBLE CROCHET

(abbreviated FPdc)

YO, insert hook from **front** to **back** around post of st indicated *(Fig. 10, page 141)*, YO and pull up a loop (3 loops on hook), (YO and draw through 2 loops on hook) twice. Skip st **behind** FPdc.

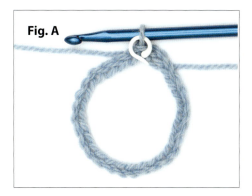

Fig. A

Fig. B

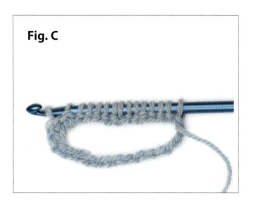

Fig. C

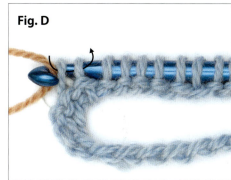

Fig. D

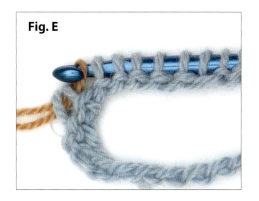

Fig. E

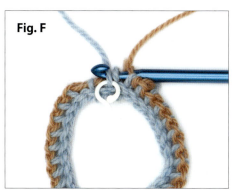

Fig. F

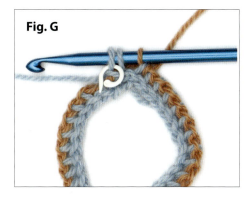

Fig. G

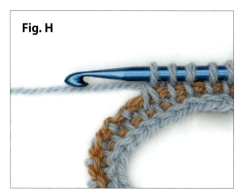

Fig. H

TUNISIAN COCOON & CAP

BODY DECREASE
Insert hook under each of next 2 bars, YO and pull up a loop *(Fig. H, page 21)* (**counts as one st**).

SINGLE CROCHET DECREASE
(**abbreviated sc2tog**)
Pull up a loop in each of next 2 sts, YO and draw through all 3 loops on hook (**counts as one sc**).

DOUBLE CROCHET 2 TOGETHER
(**abbreviated dc2tog**)
(uses next 2 sts)
★ YO, insert hook in **next** st, YO and pull up a loop, YO and draw through 2 loops on hook; repeat from ★ once **more**, YO and draw through all 3 loops on hook (counts as one dc).

FRONT POST DECREASE
(**abbreviated FP decrease**)
★ YO, insert hook from **front** to **back** around post of next dc *(Fig. 10, page 141)*, YO and pull up a loop, YO and draw through 2 loops on hook; repeat from ★ once **more**, YO and draw through all 3 loops on hook (**counts as one FPdc**).

BACK POST DECREASE
(**abbreviated BP decrease**)
★ YO, insert hook from **back** to **front** around post of next dc *(Fig. 10, page 141)*, YO and pull up a loop, YO and draw through 2 loops on hook; repeat from ★ once **more**, YO and draw through all 3 loops on hook (**counts as one BPdc**).

COCOON
Body

Use two separate skeins of Variegated yarn throughout Body which will be noted in the instructions as first yarn and second yarn.

With first yarn and using double ended hook, ch 94; being careful **not** to twist ch, join with slip st to form a ring, place marker in loop on hook to mark beginning of rnd and **right** side. Marked loop counts as first vertical bar.

Rnd 1
Step A: Working in back ridge of beginning ch *(Fig. 4, page 140)*, (insert hook in next ch, YO and pull up a loop) 46 times, leave remaining 47 chs unworked: 47 loops on hook.
Step B: Drop first yarn, turn work around; slide loops to opposite end of hook; with second yarn, (YO and draw through 2 loops on hook) across until 2 loops remain on hook.
Step C: Drop second yarn, turn work around; slide last 2 loops to opposite end of hook; with first yarn and working in back ridge of beginning ch, (insert hook in next ch, YO and pull up a loop) 47 times: 49 loops on hook.
Step D: Drop first yarn, turn work around; slide loops to opposite end of hook; with second yarn, (YO and draw through 2 loops on hook) across until 2 loops remain on hook.

Rnd 2
Step A: Drop second yarn, turn work around; slide last 2 loops to opposite end of hook; insert hook under marked vertical bar, with first yarn, YO and pull up a loop, move marker to loop just made, (insert hook under next vertical bar, YO and pull up a loop) 46 times: 49 loops on hook.
Step B: Drop first yarn, turn work around; slide loops to opposite end of hook; with second yarn, (YO and draw through 2 loops on hook) across until 2 loops remain on hook.
Step C: Drop second yarn, turn work around; slide last 2 loops to opposite end of hook, with first yarn, (insert hook under next vertical bar, YO and pull up a loop) 47 times: 49 loops on hook.
Step D: Drop first yarn, turn work around; slide loops to opposite end of hook; with second yarn, (YO and draw through 2 loops on hook) across until 2 loops remain on hook: 94 vertical bars.

Repeat Rnd 2 for pattern until Body measures approximately 22" (56 cm) from beginning ring.

Bottom

Rnd 1 (Decrease rnd)
Step A: Drop second yarn, turn work around; slide last 2 loops to opposite end of hook, with first yarn, insert hook under marked vertical bar and under next vertical bar, YO and pull up a loop (**first Body decrease made**), move marker to loop just made, (insert hook under next vertical bar, YO and pull up a loop) 23 times, work Body decrease, (insert hook under next vertical bar, YO and pull up a loop) 20 times: 47 loops on hook.
Step B: Repeat Step B of Body Rnd 2.
Step C: Drop second yarn, turn work around; slide last 2 loops to opposite end of hook; with first yarn, (insert hook under next vertical bar, YO and pull up a loop) 3 times, ★ work Body decrease, (insert hook under next vertical bar, YO and pull up a loop) 20 times; repeat from ★ once **more**: 47 loops on hook.
Step D: Drop first yarn, turn work around; slide loops to opposite end of hook; with second yarn, (YO and draw through 2 loops on hook) across until 2 loops remain on hook: 90 vertical bars.

Rnd 2 (Decrease rnd)
Step A: Drop second yarn, turn work around; slide last 2 loops to opposite end of hook; with first yarn, insert hook under marked vertical bar and under next vertical bar, YO and pull up a loop (**first Body decrease made**), move marker to loop just made, ★ (insert hook under next vertical bar, YO and pull up a loop) 13 times, work Body decrease; repeat from ★ 2 times **more**: 45 loops on hook.
Step B: Repeat Step B of Body Rnd 2.
Step C: Drop second yarn, turn work around; slide last 2 loops to opposite end of hook; with first yarn, (insert hook under next vertical bar, YO and pull up a loop) 13 times, ★ work Body decrease, (insert hook under next vertical bar, YO and pull up a loop) 13 times; repeat from ★ once **more**: 43 loops on hook.
Step D: Drop first yarn, turn work around; slide loops to opposite end of hook; with second yarn, (YO and draw through 2 loops on hook) across until 2 loops remain on hook: 84 vertical bars.

Rnds 3-12: Decrease in same manner (working 6 Body decreases per rnd), pulling up one less loop between decreases: 24 vertical bars.

Rnd 13: Work Body decrease around; cut second yarn: 12 vertical bars.

Rnd 14: (Pull up a loop under each of next 2 vertical bars, YO and draw through all 3 loops on hook) 6 times; finish off leaving a long end for sewing.

Thread yarn needle with long end and sew opening closed.

Band

Rnd 1: With right side facing, working in free loops of beginning ch (*Fig. 6b, page 140*), and using standard hook, join Blue with slip st in first ch; ch 3 (**counts as first dc, now and throughout**), dc in next 3 chs, (dc2tog, dc in next 3 chs) around; join with slip st to first dc: 76 dc.

Rnd 2: [Slip st from back to front around first dc, ch 3 (beginning BPdc made)], work FPdc around next dc, ★ work BPdc around next dc, work FPdc around next dc, work BP decrease, work FPdc around next dc, work BPdc around next dc, work FP decrease; repeat from ★ around to last 2 dc, work BPdc around next dc, work FPdc around last dc; join with slip st to first BPdc: 58 sts.

Rnds 3-10: Work beginning BPdc around beginning BPdc, work FPdc around next FPdc, (work BPdc around next BPdc, work FPdc around next FPdc) around; join with slip st to first dc; at end of Rnd 10, finish off.

Fold Band down.

TUNISIAN COCOON & CAP

HAT
Body

Use one skein each of Variegated and Blue throughout Body of Hat.

With Variegated and using double ended hook, ch 55; being careful **not** to twist ch, join with slip st to form ring, place marker in loop on hook to mark beginning of rnd and **right** side. Marked loop counts as first vertical bar.

Rnd 1

Step A: Working in back ridge of beginning ch, (insert hook in next ch, YO and pull up a loop) 27 times, leave remaining 27 chs unworked: 28 loops on hook.

Step B: Drop Variegated, turn work around; slide loops to opposite end of hook; with Blue, (YO and draw through 2 loops on hook) across until 2 loops remain on hook.

Step C: Drop Blue, turn work around; slide last 2 loops to opposite end of hook, with Variegated and working in back ridge of beginning ch, (insert hook in next ch, YO and pull up a loop) 27 times: 29 loops on hook.

Step D: Drop Variegated, turn work around; slide loops to opposite end of hook; with Blue, (YO and draw through 2 loops on hook) across until 2 loops remain on hook: 55 vertical bars.

Rnds 2-6

Step A: Drop Blue, turn work around; slide last 2 loops to opposite end of hook, insert hook under marked vertical bar; with Variegated, YO and pull up a loop, move marker to loop just made (insert hook under next vertical bar, YO and pull up a loop) 26 times: 29 loops on hook.

Step B: Drop Variegated, turn work around; slide loops to opposite end of hook; with Blue, (YO and draw through 2 loops on hook) across until 2 loops remain on hook.

Step C: Drop Blue, turn work around; slide last 2 loops to opposite end of hook; with Variegated, (insert hook under next vertical bar, YO and pull up a loop) 28 times: 30 loops on hook.

Step D: Drop Variegated, turn work around; slide loops to opposite end of hook, with Blue, (YO and draw through 2 loops on hook) across until 2 loops remain on hook: 55 vertical bars.

Rnd 7 (Decrease rnd)
Step A: Drop Blue, turn work around; slide last 2 loops to opposite end of hook; with Variegated, insert hook under marked vertical bar and under next vertical bar, YO and pull up a loop (**Body decrease made**), move marker to loop just made, ★ (insert hook under next vertical bar, YO and pull up a loop) 9 times, work Body decrease; repeat from ★ once **more**: 23 loops on hook.
Step B: Repeat Step B of Body Rnd 2.
Step C: Drop Blue, turn work around; slide last 2 loops to opposite end of hook; with Variegated, (insert hook under next vertical bar, YO and pull up a loop) 9 times, ★ work Body decrease, (insert hook under next vertical bar, YO and pull up a loop) 9 times; repeat from ★ once **more**: 31 loops on hook.
Step D: Drop Variegated, turn work around; slide loops to opposite end of hook; with Blue, (YO and draw through 2 loops on hook) across until 2 loops remain on hook: 50 vertical bars.

Rnds 8-12: Decrease in same manner (working 6 Body decreases per rnd), pulling up one less loop between decreases: 20 vertical bars.

Rnd 13: Work Body decrease around; cut Blue: 10 vertical bars.

Rnd 14: (Pull up a loop under each of next 2 vertical bars, YO and draw through all 3 loops on hook) 5 times; finish off leaving a long end for sewing.

Thread yarn needle with long end and sew opening closed.

Band
Rnd 1: With **right** side facing, working in free loops of beginning ch, and using standard hook, join Blue with sc in first ch; sc in next ch and in each ch around; do not join, place marker to mark beginning of rnd *(see Markers, page 140)*: 55 sc.

Rnd 2: (Sc in next 9 sc, sc2tog) around: 50 sc.

Rnd 3: Sc in each sc around.

Brim
Row 1 (Right side): Ch 1, turn; working in Back Loops Only *(Fig. 5, page 139)*, sc in next 16 sc, leave remaining 34 sc unworked.

Rows 2-7: Ch 1, turn; skip first sc, working in both loops, sc in next sc and in each sc across; at end of Row 7, finish off: 10 sc.

Edging: With **right** side facing, working in end of rows, and using standard hook; join Variegated with sc in first row; sc in next 5 rows, 2 sc in last row; sc in each sc across Row 7; working in end of rows, 2 sc in same row, sc in next 6 rows; ch 1, turn Hat with Body down, working in free loops of sts on Rnd 3 of Band *(Fig. 6a, page 140)*, slip st in each st around; join with slip st to first ch, finish off.

Fold Brim up.

Design by Kim Kotary.

RAINBOW CUBE

▬▬▬ ▭ ▭ EASY

Finished Size: Approximately 6½" (16.5 cm) cube

GAUGE INFORMATION
Gauge Swatch: 3" (7.5 cm) square
Work same as Square through Rnd 7: 48 sc and 4 corner ch-2 sps.

STITCH GUIDE
TREBLE CROCHET *(abbreviated tr)*
YO twice, insert hook in dc indicated, YO and pull up a loop (4 loops on hook), (YO and draw through 2 loops on hook) 3 times.

BLOCK
Square
With White, make 6 Squares.

Rnd 1 (Right side): With color indicated in individual instructions and using an adjustable loop to form a ring *(Figs. 1a-d, page 139)*, work 8 sc in ring; do **not** join, place marker to indicate beginning of rnd *(see Markers, page 140)*.

Note: Loop a short piece of yarn around any stitch to mark Rnd 1 as **right** side.

Rnd 2: (Ch 2, sc in next 2 sc) 4 times: 8 sc and 4 corner ch-2 sps.

SHOPPING LIST

Yarn
(Medium Weight)
[7 ounces, 364 yards (198 grams, 333 meters) per skein]:
☐ White - 1 skein
☐ Variegated - 50 yards (46 meters)
☐ Blue - 30 yards (27.5 meters)
☐ Yellow - 25 yards (23 meters)
☐ Dk Green - 20 yards (18.5 meters)
☐ Orange - 15 yards (13.5 meters)
☐ Red - 10 yards (9 meters)
☐ Grey - 5 yards (4.5 meters)
☐ Black - small amount

Crochet Hook
☐ Size H (5 mm)
  or size needed for gauge

Additional Supplies
☐ Yarn needle
☐ Upholstery needle
☐ Polyester fiberfill
☐ 1⅛" (28 mm) button - 1 **each** Red, Orange, Yellow, Green, **and** Blue
☐ Hole punch
☐ Flexible mirror sheet
☐ Crinkle material plastic film
☐ Linking teething rings - 6 links

Rnd 3: ★ (Sc, ch 2, sc) in next corner ch-2 sp, sc in next 2 sc; repeat from ★ around: 16 sc and 4 corner ch-2 sps.

Rnds 4-15: ★ Sc in each sc across to next corner ch-2 sp, (sc, ch 2, sc) in corner ch-2 sp; repeat from ★ around, sc in each sc across: 112 sc and 4 corner ch-2 sps.

Slip st in next sc; finish off.

JOINING
With **wrong** sides together and using Diagram as a guide on page 28 for placement, join 4 Squares to center Square as follows:

Working through **both** loops of sc on **both** pieces, join Variegated with sc in any corner ch-2 sp *(see Joining With Sc, page 138)*; sc in each sc across to next corner ch-2 sp, sc in corner ch-2 sp,

RAINBOW CUBE

★ working through **both** loops of sc on **next** Square and center Square, sc in same corner ch-2 sp as last sc on center Square and in any corner ch-2 sp on next Square, sc in each sc across to next corner ch-2 sp, sc in corner ch-2 sp; repeat from ★ 2 times **more**, ending by working last sc in same corner ch-2 sp on center Square as first sc; join with slip st to first sc, finish off.

Using remaining Square as center, repeat Joining around opposite sides of Squares.

Block Side Seam

With **wrong** sides together and working through **both** loops of sts across any unjoined edge, join Variegated with sc in any corner ch-2 sp; sc in each sc across to next corner ch-2 sp, sc in corner ch-2 sp; finish off.

Repeat Side Seam across each unjoined edge, stuffing Block with polyester fiberfill before closing.

Thread upholstery needle with a long strand of Square color yarn. Sew through middle of one Square and come out through middle of Square on opposite side of Block twice. Secure ends.

Repeat with remaining Squares of Block.

When **right** side is indicated, loop a short piece of yarn around any stitch on same row or rnd **(now and throughout)**.

Use photos as guides for placement of all pieces. For embroidery, refer to Figs. 17 and 18, page 143.

TOP
Mirror Frame

With Variegated, ch 60; being careful **not** to twist ch, join with slip st to form a ring.

Rnd 1 (Right side)**:** Ch 3 **(counts as first dc, now and throughout)**, dc in next 8 chs, 2 dc in next ch, (dc in next 9 chs, 2 dc in next ch) around; join with slip st to first dc, finish off leaving a long end.

Mirror

Using pattern below, cut a 4¼" (11 cm) diameter circle from reflective sheet, making sure it will fit under Frame. Punch 4 evenly spaced holes around edge of circle.
Sew mirror to center of one Square; then with right side facing, sew Frame in place.

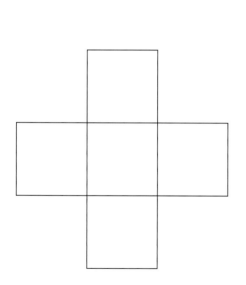

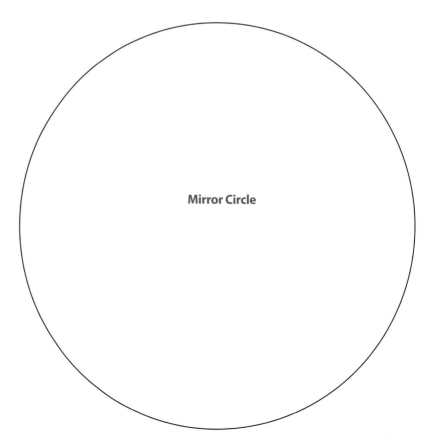

Mirror Circle

RAINBOW CUBE

SIDE 1
Rainbow

FIRST ARCH

Row 1: With Blue, ch 3, 6 dc in third ch from hook.

Row 2: Ch 3, turn; dc in same st, 2 dc in next dc and in each dc across: 12 dc.

Row 3: Ch 3, turn; 2 dc in next dc, (dc in next dc, 2 dc in next dc) across: 18 dc.

Row 4: Ch 3, turn; dc in next dc, 2 dc in next dc, (dc in next 2 dc, 2 dc in next dc) across: 24 dc.

Row 5: Ch 3, turn; dc in next 2 dc, 2 dc in next dc, (dc in next 3 dc, 2 dc in next dc) across: 30 dc.

Row 6: Ch 3, turn; dc in next 3 dc, 2 dc in next dc, (dc in next 4 dc, 2 dc in next dc) across: 36 dc.

Trim (Right side): Ch 2, do **not** turn; work 23 sc evenly spaced across ends of rows; finish off leaving a long end.

SECOND ARCH

Rows 1-5: With Green, work same as First Arch: 30 dc.

Trim (Right side): Ch 2, do not turn; work 19 sc evenly spaced across ends of rows; finish off leaving a long end.

THIRD ARCH

Rows 1-4: With Yellow, work same as First Arch: 24 dc.

Trim (Right side): Ch 2, do **not** turn; work 17 sc evenly spaced across ends of rows; finish off leaving a long end.

FOURTH ARCH

Rows 1-3: With Orange, work same as First Arch: 18 dc.

Trim (Right side): Ch 2, do **not** turn; work 13 sc evenly spaced across ends of rows; finish off leaving a long end.

FIFTH ARCH

Rows 1 and 2: With Red, work same as First Arch: 12 dc.

Trim (Right side): Ch 2, do **not** turn; work 9 sc evenly spaced across ends of rows; finish off leaving a long end.

SUN

Rnd 1 (Right side): With Yellow, ch 2, 6 sc in second ch from hook; do **not** join, place marker to indicate beginning of rnd.

Rnd 2: 2 Sc in each sc around: 12 sc.

Rnd 3: (Sc in next sc, 2 sc in next sc) around: 18 sc.

Rnd 4: (Sc in next 2 sc, 2 sc in next sc) around: 24 sc.

Slip st in next sc; finish off leaving a long end.

With Black and using straight st, add eyes and mouth to Sun.

Sew Sun to center of one Side Square. With Yellow and using straight st, add rays.

Sew bottom edge of Rainbow Arches to same Square.

29

RAINBOW CUBE

SIDE 2
Loop (Make 1 each with Red, Yellow, and Blue)

Row 1: With color indicated, work 10 fsc *(see Foundation Single Crochet, page 139).*

Rows 2 and 3: Ch 1, turn; sc in each st across.

Finish off leaving a long end.

Fold piece in half and sew short edges together.

With White and using straight st, embroider the number 1 on Red Loop, the number 2 on Yellow Loop, and the number 3 on Blue Loop.

Sew Loops to one Side Square in numerical order; then attach corresponding number of teething rings to Loops.

SIDE 3
Cloud
With Grey, ch 21.

Rnd 1 (Right side): Dc in third ch from hook and in next 17 chs, 6 dc in next ch; working in free loops of beginning ch *(Fig. 6b, page 140)*, dc in next 17 chs, 4 dc in next ch; do not join, place marker to indicate beginning of rnd: 45 dc.

Rnd 2: Slip st in next dc, sc in next dc, hdc in next dc, skip next 2 dc, 4 tr in next dc, dc in next 7 dc, 4 tr in next dc, skip next 2 dc, hdc in next dc, sc in next dc, slip st in next dc, leave remaining sts unworked.

Rnd 3 (Right side): Turn; slip st in first 7 sts, hdc in next dc, skip next 2 dc, 6 tr in next dc, skip next 2 dc, hdc in next dc, slip st in next 13 sts, sc in next dc, skip next 2 dc, 6 tr in next dc, skip next 2 dc, dc in next dc, skip next 2 dc, 6 tr in next dc, skip next 2 dc, sc in next dc, slip st in next 7 sts; join with slip st to first slip st; finish off leaving a long end.

With Black and using straight st, add eyes and mouth to Cloud.

Raindrop
BODY (Make 2 each with Red, Orange, Yellow, Dk Green, and Blue)
With color indicated, ch 5.

Rnd 1 (Right side): Slip st in second ch from hook, sc in next ch, hdc in next ch, 6 dc in next ch; working in free loops of beginning ch, hdc in next ch, sc in next ch, slip st in next ch; finish off leaving a long end on one Body of each color.

With **wrong** sides together, sew Bodies together filling with crinkle material before closing.

Join White with sc to point of Raindrop, ch 7; finish off leaving a long end.

Sew Cloud to one Side Square, filling with crinkle material before closing.

Sew Raindrops to Cloud.

SIDE 4
Heart
First Side (Right side): With Red, ch 3, 11 dc in third ch from hook, slip st in top of beginning ch, sc in next dc, (hdc, dc) in next dc, (dc, tr) in next dc; finish off leaving a long end.

Second Side (Right side): With Red, ch 3, 11 dc in third ch from hook, slip st in top of beginning ch, ch 4 **(counts as one tr)**, dc in same st, (hdc, sc) in next dc, sc in next dc, slip st in next 2 dc; finish off.

With **right** sides together, sew tr of Sides together to form point. Skip next 2 dc from point on each Side and sew next dc together.

Square
With Orange, ch 10; join with slip st to form a ring.

Rnd 1 (Right side): ★ Ch 3, 5 dc in ring, sc in top of last dc made and around same dc, sc in ring; repeat from ★ once **more**; do **not** join, place marker to indicate beginning of rnd: 18 sts.

Rnd 2: ★ Sc around next dc, (sc, ch 1, sc) in top of same dc, sc in next 4 dc, (sc, ch 1, sc) in next dc, sc in next 3 sc; repeat from ★ once more: 24 sc and 4 ch-1 sps.

Rnd 3: Sc in next 2 sc, ★ (sc, ch 1, sc) in next ch-1 sp, sc in each sc across to next ch-1 sp; repeat from ★ around to marker, remove marker, sc in each sc across to next ch-1 sp; slip st in next ch-1 sp, finish off.

Star
With Yellow, ch 15; join with slip st to form a ring.

Rnd 1 (Right side): ★ † Ch 4, sc in second ch from hook, hdc in next ch, dc in next ch, skip next 2 chs on ring †, sc in next ch; repeat from ★ 3 times **more**, then repeat from † to † once; join with slip st to joining slip st, finish off.

Triangle
Rnd 1 (Right side): With Dk Green, ch 4, ★ † sc in second ch from hook, hdc in next ch, dc in next ch †, ch 7; repeat from ★ once **more**, then repeat from † to † once, ch 3; join with slip st to free loop of ch at base of first dc: 9 sts and 3 ch-3 sps.

Rnd 2: Ch 1, working in free loops of chs, sc in same st as joining and in next 2 chs, (sc, ch 2, sc) in next ch, sc in next 3 sts, 3 sc in next ch-3 sp, ★ sc in next 3 chs, (sc, ch 2, sc) in next ch, sc in next 3 sts, 3 sc in next ch-3 sp; repeat from ★ once **more**; join with slip st first sc, finish off.

Circle
With Blue, ch 12; join with slip st to form a ring.

Rnd 1 (Right side): Ch 3, dc in same st as joining, 2 dc in next ch and in each ch around; do **not** join, place marker to indicate beginning of rnd: 24 dc.

Rnd 2: (Sc in next 2 dc, 2 sc in next dc) around; slip st in next sc, finish off.

Sew buttons to one Side Square.

BOTTOM
Slides
With Red and leaving a long end, ch 30; finish off leaving a long end.

With Orange and leaving a long end, ch 35; finish off leaving a long end.

With Yellow and leaving a long end, ch 25; finish off leaving a long end.

With Dk Green and leaving a long end, ch 15; finish off leaving a long end.

With Blue and leaving a long end, ch 30; finish off leaving a long end.

Sew Slides to last Square.

Bead (Make 5)
With Variegated, work 6 fdc *(see Foundation Double Crochet, page 139)*; finish off leaving a long end.

Wrap Bead around one Slide. Using long end, sew first and last fdc together.

Repeat for remaining Beads.

Design by Jessica Boyer.

HAT WITH FLOWER

 EASY

SIZE INFORMATION

Finished Band Circumference:

Small (3-12 months): 12" (30.5 cm)
Medium (12-18 months): 14½" (37 cm)
Large (18-24 months): 16¾" (42.5 cm)

Size Note: We have printed the instructions for the sizes in different colors to make it easier for you to find:
- Small in Blue
- Medium in Pink
- Large in Green

Instructions in Black apply to all sizes.

GAUGE INFORMATION

10 sc and 12 rows = 3" (7.5 cm)

Gauge Swatch:

2¾" (7 cm) diameter

With White, ch 4; join with slip st to form a ring.

Rnd 1 (Right side): Ch 3 **(counts as first dc, now and throughout)**, 11 dc in ring; join with slip st to first dc: 12 dc.

Rnd 2: Ch 3, dc in same st as joining, 2 dc in next dc and in each dc around; join with slip st to first dc, finish off: 24 dc.

BODY

With White, ch 4; join with slip st to form a ring.

Rnd 1 (Right side): Ch 3 **(counts as first dc, now and throughout)**, 9{11-13} dc in ring; join with slip st to first dc: 10{12-14} dc.

Note: Loop a short piece of yarn around any stitch to mark Rnd 1 as **right** side.

Rnd 2: Ch 3, dc in same st as joining, 2 dc in next dc and in each dc around; join with slip st to first dc: 20{24-28} dc.

Rnd 3: Ch 1, sc in same st as joining, ch 3, skip next dc, ★ sc in next dc, ch 3, skip next dc; repeat from ★ around; join with slip st to first sc: 10{12-14} ch-3 sps.

Rnd 4: (Slip st, ch 3, 2 dc) in next ch-3 sp, 3 dc in next ch-3 sp and in each ch-3 sp around; join with slip st to first dc: 30{36-42} dc.

Rnd 5: (Slip st, ch 1, sc) in next dc, ch 4, skip next 2 dc, ★ sc in next dc, ch 4, skip next 2 sts; repeat from ★ around; join with slip st to first sc: 10{12-14} ch-4 sps.

SHOPPING LIST

Yarn
(Medium Weight)
[3.5 ounces, 170 yards
(100 grams, 156 meters) per skein]:
☐ White - 1 skein
☐ Yellow - 1 skein

Crochet Hook
☐ Size I (5.5 mm)
   or size needed for gauge

Additional Supplies
☐ Yarn needle

Rnd 6: (Slip st, ch 3, 3 dc) in next ch-4 sp, (ch 1, 4 dc in next ch-4 sp) around, sc in first dc to form last ch-1 sp: 40{48-56} dc and 10{12-14} ch-1 sps.

Rnd 7: Ch 1, sc in last ch-1 sp made, ch 4, (2 sc in next ch-1 sp, ch 4) around, sc in same sp as first sc; join with slip st to first sc: 10{12-14} ch-4 sps.

Rnds 8 thru 9{11-13}: Repeat Rnds 6 and 7, 1{2-3} time(s): 10{12-14} ch-4 sps.

Rnd 10{12-14}: (Slip st, ch 3, 3 dc) in next ch-4 sp, ch 1, (4 dc in next ch-4 sp, ch 1) around; join with slip st to first dc, do **not** finish off: 40{48-56} dc and 10{12-14} ch-1 sps.

BAND

Rnd 1: Ch 1, sc in same st as joining and in next 3 dc, skip next ch-1 sp, (sc in next 4 dc, skip next ch-1 sp) around; join with slip st to first sc: 40{48-56} sc.

Rnds 2-4: Ch 1, sc in same st as joining and in each sc around; join with slip st to first sc.

Finish off.

FLOWER

With Yellow and leaving a long end for sewing, ch 35.

Row 1: Dc in fifth ch from hook **(4 skipped chs count as first dc plus ch 1)**, ch 1, ★ skip next ch, (dc, ch 1) twice in next ch; repeat from ★ across to last 2 chs, skip next ch, (dc, ch 1, dc) in last ch: 32 dc and 31 ch-1 sps.

Row 2 (Right side): Ch 1, turn; (sc, hdc, 2 dc, hdc, sc) in first ch-1 sp, ★ skip next ch-1 sp, (sc, hdc, 2 dc, hdc, sc) in next ch-1 sp; repeat from ★ across; finish off.

Note: Mark Row 2 as **right** side.

Thread yarn needle with beginning end and weave through beginning ch. Pull end tightly to form Flower and tack petals in place; secure end.

Using photo as a guide for placement, sew **wrong** side of Flower to **right** side of Hat.

Design by Lisa Gentry.

PLAID COCOON & CAP

 **EASY**

Finished Size
Cocoon: 24" long x 31" circumference (61 x 78.5 cm)
Hat: Fits Newborn to 3 months

GAUGE INFORMATION

In pattern,
14 sts and 15 rows = 4" (10 cm)
Gauge Swatch: 4" (10 cm) diameter
Work same as Cocoon through Rnd 8.

STITCH GUIDE

SINGLE CROCHET 2 TOGETHER
(abbreviated sc2tog)
Pull up a loop in each of next 2 sc, YO and draw through both loops on hook (**counts as one sc**).

FRONT POST DOUBLE CROCHET
(abbreviated *FPdc*)
YO, insert hook from **front** to **back** around post of FPtr indicated, YO and pull up a loop, (YO and draw through 2 loops on hook) twice *(Fig. 10, page 141)*.

FRONT POST TREBLE CROCHET
(abbreviated *FPtr*)
YO twice, insert hook from **front** to **back** around post of st indicated, YO and pull up a loop, (YO and draw through 2 loops on hook) 3 times *(Fig. 10, page 141)*. Do **not** skip sc behind FPtr unless indicated.

COCOON

Rnd 1 (Right side): With Tan, ch 2, 6 sc in second ch from hook; join with slip st to first sc.

Note: Loop a short piece of yarn around any stitch to mark Rnd 1 as **right** side.

Rnd 2: Ch 1, 2 sc in Back Loop Only of each sc around *(Fig. 5, page 140)*; join with slip st to first ch, drop Tan to **wrong** side: 12 sc.

Carry unused yarn on **wrong** side of piece.

Rnd 3: With Brown, ch 1, sc in Back Loop Only of first sc, working in **front** of previous rnd *(Fig. 9, page 141)*, dc in free loop of first sc on Rnd 1 *(Fig. 6a, page 140)*, ★ sc in Back Loop Only of next 2 sc, working in front of previous rnd, dc in free loop of next sc on Rnd 1; repeat from ★ around to last sc, sc in Back Loop Only of last sc; join with slip st to first ch: 12 sc and 6 dc.

SHOPPING LIST

Yarn
(Medium Weight) **4**
[3.5 ounces, 200 yards
(100 grams, 182 meters)
per skein]:
☐ Tan - 3 skeins
☐ Brown - 3 skeins

Crochet Hook
☐ Size H (5 mm)
  or size needed for gauge

Additional Supplies
☐ Yarn needle

PLAID COCOON & CAP

Rnd 4: Ch 1, working in Back Loops Only, sc in first sc, 2 sc in next dc, (sc in next 2 sc, 2 sc in next dc) around to last sc, sc in last sc; join with slip st to first ch, drop Brown: 24 sc.

Rnd 5: With Tan, ch 1, sc in Back Loop Only of first 4 sc, working in **front** of previous rnd, dc in free loop of next sc on Rnd 2, ★ sc in Back Loop Only of next 4 sc, working in **front** of previous rnd, dc in free loop of next sc on Rnd 2 repeat from ★ around; join with slip st to first ch: 24 sc and 6 dc.

Continue to work sc in Back Loops Only of sts on previous rnd.

Rnd 6: Ch 1, sc in first 4 sc, 2 sc in next dc, (sc in next 4 sc, 2 sc in next dc) around; join with slip st to first ch, drop Tan: 36 sc.

Rnd 7: With Brown, ch 1, sc in first 2 sc, work FPtr around next dc 4 rnds **below**, (sc in next 6 sc, work FPtr around next dc 4 rnds **below**) around to last 4 sc, sc in last 4 sc; join with slip st to first ch: 36 sc and 6 FPtr.

Rnd 8: Ch 1, sc in first 2 sc, 2 sc in next FPtr, (sc in next 6 sc, 2 sc in next FPtr) around to last 4 sc, sc in last 4 sc; join with slip st to first ch, drop Brown: 48 sc.

Rnd 9: With Tan, ch 1, sc in first 7 sc, work FPtr around next dc 4 rnds **below**, (sc in next 8 sc, work FPtr around next dc 4 rnds **below**) around to last sc, sc in last sc; join with slip st to first ch: 48 sc and 6 FPtr.

Rnd 10: Ch 1, sc in first 7 sc, 2 sc in next FPtr, (sc in next 8 sc, 2 sc in next FPtr) around to last sc, sc in last sc; join with slip st to first ch, drop Tan: 60 sc.

Work FPtr around FPtr 4 rnds **below** throughout, unless otherwise indicated.

Rnd 11: With Brown, ch 1, sc in first 3 sc, work FPtr around next FPtr, (sc in next 10 sc, work FPtr around next FPtr) around to last 7 sc, sc in last 7 sc; join with slip st to first ch: 60 sc and 6 FPtr.

Rnd 12: Ch 1, sc in first 3 sc, 2 sc in next FPtr, (sc in next 10 sc, 2 sc in next FPtr) around to last 7 sc, sc in last 7 sc; join with slip st to first ch, drop Brown: 72 sc.

Rnd 13: With Tan, ch 1, sc in first 10 sc, work FPtr around next FPtr, (sc in next 12 sc, work FPtr around next FPtr) around to last 2 sc, sc in last 2 sc; join with slip st to first ch: 72 sc and 6 FPtr.

Rnd 14: Ch 1, sc in first 10 sc, 2 sc in next FPtr, (sc in next 12 sc, 2 sc in next FPtr) around to last 2 sc, sc in last 2 sc; join with slip st to first ch, drop Tan: 84 sc.

Rnd 15: With Brown, ch 1, sc in first 4 sc, work FPtr around next FPtr, (sc in next 14 sc, work FPtr around next FPtr) around to last 10 sc, sc in last 10 sc; join with slip st to first ch: 84 sc and 6 FPtr.

Rnd 16: Ch 1, sc in first 4 sc, 2 sc in next FPtr, (sc in next 14 sc, 2 sc in next FPtr) around to last 10 sc, sc in last 10 sc; join with slip st to first ch, drop Brown: 96 sc.

Rnd 17: With Tan, ch 1, sc in first 13 sc, work FPtr around next FPtr, (sc in next 16 sc, work FPtr around next FPtr) around to last 3 sc, sc in last 3 sc; join with slip st to first ch: 96 sc and 6 FPtr.

Rnd 18: Ch 1, sc in first 13 sc, 2 sc in next FPtr, (sc in next 16 sc, 2 sc in next FPtr) around to last 3 sc, sc in last 3 sc; join with slip st to first ch, drop Tan: 108 sc.

Rnd 19: With Brown, ch 1, sc in first 5 sc, work FPtr around next FPtr, skip sc behind FPtr just made, ★ sc in next 17 sc, work FPtr around next FPtr, skip sc behind FPtr just made; repeat from ★ around to last 12 sc, sc in last 12 sc; join with slip st to first ch: 102 sc and 6 FPtr.

Rnd 20: Ch 1, sc in each st around; join with slip st to first ch, drop Brown: 108 sc.

Rnd 21: With Tan, ch 1, sc in first 14 sc, work FPtr around next FPtr, skip sc behind FPtr just made, ★ sc in next 17 sc, work FPtr around next FPtr, skip sc behind FPtr just made; repeat from ★ around to last 3 sc, sc in last 3 sc; join with slip st to first ch: 102 sc and 6 FPtr.

Rnd 22: Ch 1, sc in each st around; join with slip st to first ch, drop Tan: 108 sc.

Repeat Rnds 19-22 until piece measures approximately 22" (56 cm) from beginning, or to 2" (5 cm) less than desired length, ending by working Rnd 21.

Next Rnd: Ch 1, sc in first 14 sc, work FPdc around next FPtr, ★ sc in next 17 sc, work FPdc around next FPtr; repeat from ★ around to last 3 sc, sc in last 3 sc; join with slip st to first ch, cut Tan.

Last Rnd: With Brown, ch 1, sc in first 5 sc, work FPtr around next FPtr, skip sc behind FPtr just made, ★ sc in next 17 sts, work FPtr around next FPtr, skip sc behind FPtr just made; repeat from ★ around to last 12 sc, sc in last 12 sc; join with slip st to first ch, finish off leaving a long end for sewing.

Cuff

Row 1 (Right side): With Tan, ch 2, [insert hook in second ch from hook, YO and pull up a loop, YO and draw through one loop on hook (**ch made**), YO and draw through both loops on hook (**sc made**)], work 24 fsc: 25 sc.

Row 2: Ch 1, turn; working in Back Loops Only, sc in first sc, ★ insert hook in same st as previous st, YO and pull up a loop, insert hook in next st, YO and draw through st and both loops on hook; repeat from ★ across to last sc, sc in last sc, drop Tan.

Rows 3 and 4: With Brown, repeat Row 2 twice; at end of Row 4, drop Brown.

Rows 5 and 6: With Tan, repeat Row 2 twice.

Repeat Rows 3-6 until Cuff measures same as top edge of Cocoon, ending by working Row 4.

Cut Tan and finish off Brown, leaving a long end for sewing; whipstitch ends together (*Fig. 13c, page 142*). Thread yarn needle with long end on Cocoon and sew end of rows of Cuff to last rnd of Cocoon. Fold Cuff down.

CAP
Side (Make 2)

Work same as Cocoon through Rnd 10: 60 sc.

Begin working in rows.

Row 1 (Right side): With Brown, ch 1, working in Back Loops Only, sc in first 3 sc, work FPtr around next FPtr, (sc in next 10 sc, work FPtr around next FPtr) 3 times, sc in next 3 sc, leave last 24 sc unworked: 36 sc and 4 FPtr.

Row 2: Ch 1, turn; sc in Front Loop Only of each st across, drop Brown: 40 sc.

Row 3: With Tan, ch 1, turn; working Back Loops Only, sc in first 9 sc, work FPtr around next FPtr, skip sc behind FPtr just made, ★ sc in next 10 sc, work FPtr around next FPtr, skip sc behind FPtr just made; repeat from ★ once **more**, sc in last 8 sc: 37 sc and 3 FPtr.

Row 4: Ch 1, turn; sc in Front Loop Only of each st across, drop Tan: 40 sc.

Row 5: With Brown, ch 1, turn; working In Back Loops Only, sc in first 3 sc, work FPtr around next FPtr, skip sc behind FPtr just made, ★ sc in next 10 sc, work FPtr around next FPtr, skip sc behind FPtr just made; repeat from ★ 2 times **more**, sc in last 3 sc: 36 sc and 4 FPtr.

Row 6: Ch 1, turn; sc in Front Loop Only of each st across; cut Brown: 40 sc.

Row 7: Repeat Row 3; finish off leaving a long end for sewing.

With **wrong** sides together, whipstitch Row 7 of both pieces together, matching sts and working through **inside** loops only.

Edging & Ties

With **wrong** side facing, join Brown with slip st in end of first row of Side; ch 1, work 11 sc evenly spaced across end of rows, turn; working in Back Loops Only, sc2tog, (sc in next sc, sc2tog) 3 times, † working in unworked sts on Rnd 10, sc in next 7 sc, work FPtr around next FPtr, skip sc **behind** FPtr just made, sc in next 4 sc, [insert hook in next sc, YO and pull up a loop, YO and draw through one loop on hook (**ch made**), YO and draw through both loops on hook (**sc made**)], work 29 fsc; working in chs across opposite side, 2 sc in first ch, sc in each ch across; working in unworked sts on Rnd 10, sc in next 4 sc, work FPtr around next FPtr, skip sc behind FPtr just made, sc in next 6 sc †; work 15 sc evenly spaced across end of rows; repeat from † to † once; join with slip st to next sc, finish off.

Design by Kim Kotary.

WASHCLOTH

 EASY

Finished Size: Approximately 7" (18

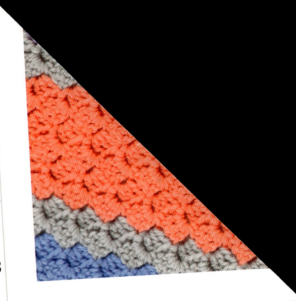

GAUGE INFORMATION
Gauge is not of great importance; your washcloth may be a bit larger or smaller without changing the overall effect.

WASHCLOTH
You can make the washcloth with only one color or with two colors, using one of the colors for the Body and the other color for the Edging.

BODY
With first color, ch 30.

Row 1: Sc in second ch from hook, ★ ch 1, skip next ch, sc in next ch; repeat from ★ across: 15 sc and 15 chs.

Row 2: Ch 1, place marker in ch just made, turn; skip first sc, ★ sc in next ch-1 sp, ch 1, skip next sc; repeat from ★ across, sc in marked ch, remove marker: 15 sc and 15 chs.

Repeat Row 2 for pattern until Body measures approximately 7" (18 cm) from beginning ch.

EDGING
Same Color Edging
Ch 1, turn; 2 sc in first sc, sc in each ch-1 sp and in each sc across to turning ch, 2 sc in turning ch; sc in end of each row across; working in free loops of beginning ch *(Fig. 6b, page 140)*, 2 sc in first ch, sc in each ch across to corner, 2 sc in corner; sc in end of each row across; join with slip st to first sc, finish off.

Contrasting Color Edging
Finish off. Turn work and join second color with slip st in first sc; ch 1, 2 sc in same st, sc in each ch-1 sp and in each sc across to turning ch, 2 sc in turning ch; sc in end of each row across; working in free loops of beginning ch *(Fig. 6b, page 140)*, 2 sc in first ch, sc in each ch across to corner, 2 sc in corner; sc in end of each row across; join with slip st to first sc, finish off.

Design by Sharon H. Silverman.

SHOPPING LIST

Yarn
(Medium Weight Cotton) [4]
[2.5 ounces, 120 yards
(71 grams, 109 meters)
per skein]:
☐ Solid - 1 skein
[2 ounces, 95 yards,
(57 grams, 86 meters) per skein]
☐ Ombre - 1 skein
Note: Two skeins will make four washcloths: two solid color with an ombre edging and two ombre with a solid edging.

Crochet Hook
☐ Size H (5 mm)

Additional Supplies
☐ Removable markers **or** scrap yarn
☐ Yarn needle

TRADITIONAL CAR SEAT COVER

 EASY

Finished Size: 17½" x 22½" (44.5 cm x 57 cm)

GAUGE INFORMATION
4 Blocks (side by side) = 3" (7.5 cm)
Gauge Swatch: 3" x 3" x 4"
   (7.5 cm x 7.5 cm x 10 cm)
Work same as Body for 4 rows: 4 Blocks.

STITCH GUIDE
BEGINNING BLOCK
Ch 6, turn; dc in fourth ch from hook and in next 2 chs.
BLOCK
Slip st in ch-3 sp of previous Block *(Fig. A, page 90)*, ch 3, 3 dc in same sp *(Fig. B, page 90)*.

BODY
Body is worked diagonally.

Row 1 (Right side): With Grey, ch 6, dc in fourth ch from hook and in last 2 chs: one Block.

Row 2: Work Beginning Block, slip st in ch-3 sp on first Block, ch 3, 3 dc in same sp: 2 Blocks.

Row 3: Work Beginning Block, slip st in ch-3 sp on first Block, ch 3, 3 dc in same sp, work Block: 3 Blocks.

Row 4: Work Beginning Block, slip st in ch-3 sp on first Block, ch 3, 3 dc in same sp, work Blocks across changing to Blue in last dc *(Fig. 7d, page 140)*; cut Grey: 4 Blocks.

Rows 5-9: Work Beginning Block, slip st in ch-3 sp on first Block, ch 3, 3 dc in same sp, work Blocks across: 9 Blocks.

Row 10: Work Beginning Block, slip st in ch-3 sp on first Block, ch 3, 3 dc in same sp, work Blocks across changing to Grey in last dc; cut Blue: 10 Blocks.

Row 11: Work Beginning Block, slip st in ch-3 sp on first Block, ch 3, 3 dc in same sp, work Blocks across: 11 Blocks.

Row 12: Work Beginning Block, slip st in ch-3 sp on first Block, ch 3, 3 dc in same sp, work Blocks across changing to Peach in last dc; cut Grey: 12 Blocks.

SHOPPING LIST

Yarn
(Light Weight) [3]
[4.5 ounces, 318 yards
(127 grams, 290 meters)
per skein]:
☐ Grey - 1 skein
☐ Lilac - 1 skein
☐ Peach - 1 skein
☐ Green - 1 skein
☐ Blue - 1 skein

Crochet Hook
☐ Size H (5 mm)
   or size needed for gauge

TRADITIONAL CAR SEAT COVER

Rows 13-17: Work Beginning Block, slip st in ch-3 sp on first Block, ch 3, 3 dc in same sp, work Blocks across: 17 Blocks.

Row 18: Work Beginning Block, slip st in ch-3 sp on first Block, ch 3, 3 dc in same sp, work Blocks across changing to Grey in last dc; cut Peach: 18 Blocks.

Row 19: Work Beginning Block, slip st in ch-3 sp on first Block, ch 3, 3 dc in same sp, work Blocks across: 19 Blocks.

Row 20: Work Beginning Block, slip st in ch-3 sp on first Block, ch 3, 3 dc in same sp, work Blocks across changing to Purple in last dc; cut Grey: 20 Blocks.

Rows 21-25: Work Beginning Block, slip st in ch-3 sp on first Block, ch 3, 3 dc in same sp, work Blocks across: 25 Blocks.

Row 26: Work Beginning Block, slip st in ch-3 sp on first Block, ch 3, 3 dc in same sp, work Blocks across changing to Grey in last dc; cut Purple: 26 Blocks.

Row 27: Work Beginning Block, slip st in ch-3 sp on first Block, ch 3, 3 dc in same sp, work Blocks across: 27 Blocks.

Row 28: Turn; slip st in first 3 dc and in next ch-3 sp, ch 3, 3 dc in same sp, work Blocks across changing to Green in last dc; cut Grey.

Row 29: Work Beginning Block, slip st in ch-3 sp on first Block, ch 3, 3 dc in same sp, work Blocks across to last Block, slip st in ch-3 sp on last Block.

Row 30: Turn; slip st in first 3 dc and in next ch-3 sp, ch 3, 3 dc in same sp, work Blocks across.

Rows 31-33: Repeat Rows 29 and 30 once, then repeat Row 29 once **more**.

Row 34: Turn; slip st in first 3 dc and in next ch-3 sp, ch 3, 3 dc in same sp, work Blocks across changing to Grey in last dc; cut Green.

Rows 35 and 36: Repeat Rows 29 and 30.

Row 37: Turn; slip st in first 3 dc and in next ch-3 sp changing to Purple in last slip st made; cut Grey, ch 3, 3 dc in same sp, work Blocks across to last Block, slip st in ch-3 sp on last Block: 26 Blocks.

Rows 38-42: Turn; slip st in first 3 dc and in next ch-3 sp, ch 3, 3 dc in same sp, work Blocks across to last Block, slip st in ch-3 sp on last Block: 21 Blocks.

Row 43 (Decrease row)**:** Turn; slip st in first 3 dc and in next ch-3 sp changing to Grey in last slip st made; cut old color, ch 3, 3 dc in same sp, work Blocks across to last Block, slip st in ch-3 sp on last Block: 20 Blocks.

Row 44 (Decrease row)**:** Turn; slip st in first 3 dc and in next ch-3 sp, ch 3, 3 dc in same sp, work Blocks across to last Block, slip st in ch-3 sp on last Block: 19 Blocks.

Row 45: Turn; slip st in first 3 dc and in next ch-3 sp changing to Peach in last slip st made; cut Grey, ch 3, 3 dc in same sp, work Blocks across to last Block, slip st in ch-3 sp on last Block: 18 Blocks.

Rows 46-50: Repeat Row 44, 5 times: 13 Blocks.

Rows 51 and 52: Repeat Rows 43 and 44: 11 Blocks.

Row 53: Turn; slip st in first 3 dc and in next ch-3 sp changing to Blue in last slip st made; cut Grey, ch 3, 3 dc in same sp, work Blocks across to last Block, slip st in ch-3 sp on last Block: 10 Blocks.

Rows 54-58: Repeat Row 44, 5 times: 5 Blocks.

Row 59: Repeat Row 43: 4 Blocks.

Row 60: Turn; slip st in first 3 dc and in next ch-3 sp, ch 3, 3 dc in same sp, work 2 Blocks, slip st in ch-3 sp on last Block: 3 Blocks.

Row 61: Turn; slip st in first 3 dc and in next ch-3 sp, ch 3, 3 dc in same sp, work Block, slip st in ch-3 sp on last Block: 2 Blocks.

Row 62: Turn; slip st in first 3 dc and in next ch-3 sp, ch 3, 3 dc in same sp, slip st in ch-3 sp on last Block; do **not** finish off: one Block.

EDGING

Rnd 1: Ch 1, turn; sc evenly around entire Body, working 3 sc in each corner; join with slip st to first sc.

Rnd 2: Ch 1, working from **left** to **right**, work reverse sc in each sc around *(Figs. 12a-d, page 141)*; join with slip st to first sc, finish off.

Design by Becky Stevens.

RIBBED COLLAR SWEATER

 EASY

SIZE INFORMATION

Size	Finished Chest Measurement	
6 months	21½"	(54.5 cm)
12 months	23¾"	(60.5 cm)
24 months	26"	(66 cm)

Size Note: We have printed the instructions for the sizes in different colors to make it easier for you to find:
- Size 6 months in Blue
- Size 12 months in Pink
- Size 24 months in Green

Instructions in Black apply to all sizes.

GAUGE INFORMATION

14 sc and 16 rows = 4" (10 cm)
Gauge Swatch: 4" (10 cm) square
With Teal, ch 15.
Row 1: Sc in back ridge of second ch from hook *(Fig. 4, page 140)* and in each ch across: 14 sc.
Rows 2-16: Ch 1, turn; sc in each sc across. Finish off.

STITCH GUIDE

SINGLE CROCHET 3 TOGETHER
(abbreviated sc3tog) (uses next 3 sts)
Pull up a loop in each of next 3 sts, YO and draw through all 4 loops on hook **(counts as one sc).**

Work stripes as desired by changing colors at the ends of rows *(Fig. 7b, page 140)*.

BODY

With Navy, ch 130{142-154}.

Row 1: Working in back ridge of beginning ch *(Fig. 4, page 140)*, sc in second ch from hook and in next 28{30-32} chs, sc3tog, place split-ring marker in sc just made, sc in next 65{73-81} chs, sc3tog, place split-ring marker in sc just made, sc in last 29{31-33} chs: 125{137-149} sc.

Row 2 (Right side): Ch 1, turn; ★ sc in each sc across to within one sc of marked sc, sc3tog, move marker to sc just made; repeat from ★ once **more**, sc in each sc across: 121{133-145} sc.

Note: Loop a short piece of yarn around any stitch to mark Row 2 as **right** side.

Rows 3 thru 16{18-20}: Ch 1, turn; ★ sc in each sc across to within one sc of marked sc, sc3tog, move marker to sc just made; repeat from ★ once **more**, sc in each sc across: 65{69-73} sc.

SHOPPING LIST

Yarn
(Medium Weight)
[3.5 ounces, 200 yards (100 grams, 182 meters) per skein]:
☐ Blue - 2 skeins
☐ White 1 skein
☐ Navy - 1 skein

Crochet Hook
☐ Size H (5 mm)
  or size needed for gauge

Additional Supplies
☐ Split-ring stitch markers - 2
☐ Yarn needle
☐ Sewing needle and thread
☐ ½" (12 mm) Buttons - 3

RIBBED COLLAR SWEATER

Row 17{19-21}: Ch 1, turn; ★ sc in each st across to marked sc, 3 sc in marked sc, remove marker; repeat from ★ once more, sc in each sc across: 69{73-77} sc.

Rows 18{20-22} thru 30{34-36}: Ch 1, turn; sc in each sc across working 3 sc in center sc of each 3-sc group: 121{133-137} sc.

Finish off.

Neck Shaping

Row 1: With **wrong** side facing, skip first 6{7-8} sc and join yarn with sc in next sc *(see Joining With Sc, page 138)*; ★ sc in each sc across to center sc of next 3-sc group, 3 sc in center sc; repeat from ★ once **more**, sc in each sc across to last 6{7-8} sc, leave last 6{7-8} sc unworked: 113{123-125} sc.

Rows 2 thru 4{6-8}: Ch 1, turn; ★ sc in each sc across to center sc of next 3-sc group, 3 sc in center sc; repeat from ★ once **more**, sc in each sc across: 125{143-153} sc.

Buttonhole Row - Boys Only: Ch 1, turn; ★ sc in each sc across to center sc of next 3-sc group, 3 sc in center sc; repeat from ★ once **more**, sc in each sc across to last 14 sc, (ch 1, skip next sc, sc in next 5 sc) twice, ch 1, skip next sc, sc in last sc: 126{144-154} sc and 3 ch-1 sps.

Buttonhole Row - Girls Only: Ch 1, turn; sc in first sc, (ch 1, skip next sc, sc in next 5 sc) twice, ★ sc in each sc across to center sc of next 3-sc group, 3 sc in center sc; repeat from ★ once **more**, sc in each sc across: 126{144-154} sc and 3 ch-1 sps.

Last Row: Ch 1, turn; sc in each sc and in each ch-1 sp across working 3 sc in center sc of each 3-sc group; finish off: 133{151-161} sc.

With **wrong** side facing and Navy, sew each shoulder/sleeve seam from last row of Body to wrist *(see How to Fold & Sew, page 144)*.

COLLAR

Row 1: With **right** side facing, join White with sc in last row of Neck Shaping on right front; sc in next 5{7-9} rows, sc in next 6{7-8} sc; working in free loops of beginning ch *(Fig. 6b, page 140)*, work 14{16-18} sc evenly spaced across; sc in next 6{7-8} sc; sc in next 6{8-10} rows; finish off: 38{46-54} sc.

Row 2: With **right** side facing, skip first 3 sc on Row 1 and join White with sc in next sc; sc in next 7{10-13} sc, 2 sc in each of next 2 sc, sc in next 12{14-16} sc, 2 sc in each of next 2 sc, sc in next 8{11-14} sc, leave last 3 sc unworked: 36{44-52} sc.

Row 3: Ch 9, turn; sc in second ch from hook and in each ch across; slip st in first 2 sc on Row 2.

Row 4: Ch 1, turn; skip first 2 slip sts, sc in Back Loop Only of next 8 sc *(Fig. 5, page 140)*.

Row 5: Ch 1, turn; sc in Back Loop Only of first 8 sc; slip st in next 2 sc on Row 2.

Repeat Rows 4 and 5, 16{20-24} times; then repeat Row 4 once **more**; finish off.

SLEEVE AND CUFF

Rnd 1: With **right** side of one sleeve facing and working in free loops of beginning ch, join yarn with sc at bottom edge; work 26{29-32} sc evenly spaced around; join with slip st to first sc: 27{30-33} sc.

Rnd 2: Ch 1, sc in first sc, pull up a loop in each of next 2 sc, YO and draw through all 3 loops on hook **(counts as one sc)**, ★ sc in next sc, pull up a loop in each of next 2 sc, YO and draw through all 3 loops on hook **(counts as one sc)**; repeat from ★ around; join with slip st to first sc, finish off: 18{20-22} sc.

Begin working in rows.

Row 1: With **right** side facing, join White with slip st in first sc; ch 9{13-17}, turn; sc in second ch from hook and in each ch across; slip st in same st as joining slip st and in next sc on Rnd 2.

Row 2: Ch 1, turn; skip first 2 slip sts, sc in Back Loop Only of next 8{12-16} sc.

Row 3: Ch 1, turn; sc in Back Loop Only of first 8{12-16} sc; slip st in next 2 sc on Rnd 2.

Repeat Rows 2 and 3, 7{8-9} times; then repeat Row 2 once **more**.

Finish off leaving a long end for sewing.

With **right** sides of Row 1 and last row together, sew Cuff seam.

Repeat for remaining sleeve.

Sew buttons to front opposite buttonholes.

Design by Darla Sims.

CIRCLES BLANKET

 EASY

Finished Size: 38" wide x 50" high (96.5 cm x 127 cm)

GAUGE INFORMATION
Each Square = 6" (15 cm)
Gauge Swatch: 2⅛" (5.4 cm) square
Work same as Square through Rnd 2: 32 dc.

STITCH GUIDE
TREBLE CROCHET *(abbreviated tr)*
YO twice, insert hook in sc indicated, YO and pull up a loop (4 loops on hook), (YO and draw through 2 loops on hook) 3 times.

BLUE SQUARE (Make 8)
With Blue, ch 4; join with slip st to form a ring.

Rnd 1 (Right side)**:** Ch 3 **(counts as first dc, now and throughout)**, 15 dc in ring; join with slip st to first dc, finish off: 16 dc.

Note: Loop a short piece of yarn around any stitch to mark Rnd 1 as **right** side.

Rnd 2: With **right** side facing, join White with dc in any dc *(see Joining With Dc, page 139)*; dc in same st, 2 dc in next dc and in each dc around; join with slip st to first dc, finish off: 32 dc.

Rnd 3: With **right** side facing, join Blue with dc in any dc; dc in same st and in next dc, (2 dc in next dc, dc in next dc) around; join with slip st to first dc, finish off: 48 dc.

Rnd 4: With **right** side facing, join White with dc in any dc; dc in same st and in next 2 dc, (2 dc in next dc, dc in next 2 dc) around; join with slip st to first dc, finish off: 64 dc.

Rnd 5: With **right** side facing, join Blue with sc in any dc *(see Joining With Sc, page 138)*; (ch 5, skip next 3 dc, sc in next dc) around to last 3 dc, ch 2, skip last 3 dc, dc in first sc to form last ch-5 sp: 16 sc and 16 ch-5 sps.

Rnd 6: Ch 1, 3 sc in last sp made, 5 sc in next ch-5 sp and in each ch-5 sp around, 2 sc in same sp as first sc; join with slip st to first sc: 80 sc.

Rnd 7: Ch 4 **(counts as first tr)**, ★ † tr in next 2 sc, dc in next 2 sc, hdc in next 2 sc, sc in next 7 sc, hdc in next 2 sc, dc in next 2 sc, tr in next 2 sc †, (tr, ch 3, tr) in next sc; repeat from ★ 2 times **more**, then repeat from † to † once, tr in same st as first tr, ch 1, hdc in first tr to form last corner ch-3 sp: 84 sts and 4 ch-3 sps.

SHOPPING LIST

Yarn
(Light Weight)
[5 ounces, 395 yards (140 grams, 361 meters) per skein]:
☐ White - 2 skeins
☐ Blue - 1 skein
☐ Green - 1 skein
☐ Lilac - 1 skein
☐ Mint - 1 skein
☐ Pink - 1 skein
☐ Yellow - 1 skein

Crochet Hook
☐ Size G (4 mm)
   or size needed for gauge

Additional Supplies
☐ Yarn needle

Rnd 8: Ch 3, dc in last corner sp made and in next 21 sts, ★ (2 dc, ch 2, 2 dc) in next corner ch-3 sp, dc in next 21 sts; repeat from ★ 2 times **more**, 2 dc in same sp as first dc, ch 1, sc in first dc to form last corner ch-2 sp; finish off leaving a long end for sewing: 100 dc and 4 ch-2 sps.

REMAINING SQUARES
(Make 40)

Replacing Blue with new color, make 8 each using the following colors: Green, Lilac, Mint, Pink, Yellow.

ASSEMBLY

With **wrong** sides together, working through **inside** loops, and using long end, whipstitch Squares together in random order *(Fig. 13b, page 142)*, forming 6 vertical strips of 8 Squares each, beginning in second st of corner ch-2 and ending in first st of next corner ch-2; then whipstitch Strips together in same manner.

EDGING

With **right** side facing, join White with dc in any st; dc evenly around working 3 dc in each dc corner; join with slip st to first dc, finish off.

Design by Melissa Leapman.

TWINKLE TWINKLE STROLLER BLANKET

 EASY

Finished Size: 20" x 30" (51 cm x 76 cm)

GAUGE INFORMATION

11 sc and 14 rows = 3½" (9 cm)
Gauge Swatch: 3½" (9 cm) square
With Navy, ch 12.
Row 1: Sc in second ch from hook and in each ch across: 11 sc.
Rows 2-14: Ch 1, turn; sc in each sc across.
Finish off.

STITCH GUIDE

TREBLE CROCHET *(abbreviated tr)*
YO twice, insert hook in st indicated, YO and pull up a loop (4 loops on hook), (YO and draw through 2 loops on hook) 3 times.

BODY

Each row is worked across length of afghan.

Star Section

Row 1: With Navy, work 78 fsc.

Row 2 (Right side): Ch 1, turn; sc in first sc, being careful to keep all the loops the same height, pull up a loop in side of sc just made and in same sc, pull up a loop in next 2 sc *(Fig. A)*, YO and draw through all 5 loops on hook, ch 1 for eye (**first Star St made**), ★ pull up a loop in eye of Star St just made and in last loop at side of Star St, pull up a loop in same sc as last loop and in next 2 sc, YO and draw through all 6 loops on hook, ch 1 for eye (**Star St made**); repeat from ★ across to last sc, sc in last sc: 38 Star Sts and 2 sc.

Fig. A

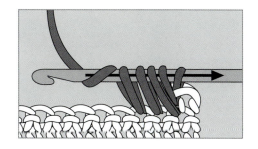

Note: Loop a short piece of yarn around any stitch to mark Row 2 as **right** side.

SHOPPING LIST

Yarn
(Medium Weight) [4]
[3.5 ounces, 170 yards
(100 grams, 156 meters)
per skein]:
☐ Yellow - 2 skeins
☐ Navy - 2 skeins

Crochet Hook
☐ Size J (6 mm)
  or size needed for gauge

Additional Supplies
☐ Safety pins - 2
☐ Yarn needle

TWINKLE TWINKLE STROLLER BLANKET

Row 3: Ch 1, turn; sc in first sc, (sc in next eye and in next Star St) across to last sc, sc in last sc: 78 sc.

Row 4: Ch 1, turn; sc in first sc, work Star Sts across to last sc, sc in last sc: 38 Star Sts and 2 sc.

Repeat Rows 3 and 4 until Star Section measures approximately 6½" (16.5 cm), ending by working Row 3.

Finish off.

Cording

Row 1: With **wrong** side facing, join Yellow with slip st in first sc; ch 1, sc in same st and in each sc across.

Rows 2-4: Ch 1, turn, sc in each sc across.

Row 5 (Cording row): Ch 1, turn; push first 4 rows to the **right** side, working through horizontal bar of sc on Row 1 **AND** in both loops of sc on Row 4, dc in each st across; do **not** finish off.

Striped Section

Row 1 (Right side): Ch 2, turn; dc in first dc, ★ skip next dc, dc in next dc, working around dc just made *(Fig. 11a & b, page 141)*, dc in skipped dc **(Cross St made)**; repeat from ★ across to last dc, dc in last dc; place loop from hook onto safety pin to keep piece from unraveling while working next row: 38 Cross Sts and 2 dc.

Row 2 (Right side): Return to beginning of Row 1 and join Navy with slip st in first dc; ch 1, sc in same st and in each dc across; place loop from hook onto safety pin: 78 sc.

Row 3: Place Yellow loop onto hook, turn; slip st in first sc, ch 2, dc in same st, ★ skip next sc, dc in next sc, working **around** dc just made, dc in skipped sc; repeat from ★ across to last sc, dc in last sc; place loop from hook onto safety pin: 38 Cross Sts and 2 dc.

Row 4: Place Navy loop onto hook, slip st in first dc, ch 1, sc in same st and in each dc across; place loop from hook onto safety pin: 78 sc.

Rows 5-26: Repeat Rows 3 and 4, 11 times.

Row 27 (Wrong side): Repeat Row 3; do **not** place loop onto safety pin, finish off Yellow.

Row 28 (Wrong side): Repeat Row 4; do **not** place loop onto safety pin or finish off.

Body Edging

Rnd 1 (Right side): Ch 1, turn; 3 sc in first sc, sc in next sc and in each sc across to last sc, 3 sc in last sc; sc evenly across end of rows; working in ch at base of each fsc, 3 sc in first ch, sc in each ch across to last ch, 3 sc in last ch; sc evenly across end of rows; join with slip st to first sc.

Rnd 2: Ch 2, do **not** turn; hdc in each sc around working 3 hdc in center sc of each corner 3-sc group; join with slip st to first hdc, finish off.

POCKET

Row 1: With Navy, work 58 fsc.

Row 2: Ch 1, turn; sc in each sc across.

Repeat Row 2 until Pocket measures approximately 11½" (29 cm); finish off.

Pocket Edging

Row 1 (Right side): Working in end of rows, join Yellow with slip st in Row 1; ch 1, sc evenly across; working across last row, 3 sc in first sc, sc in next sc and in each sc across to last sc, 3 sc in last sc; sc evenly across end of rows.

Rows 2 and 3: Ch 2, turn; hdc in first st and in each st across working 3 hdc in center st of each corner 3-st group.

Finish off.

ASSEMBLY

Using photo as a guide, place **wrong** side of Pocket and **right** side of Body together matching foundation edge of Pocket (edge without Edging) with end of rows on Body. Working through both thicknesses, join Navy with slip st in corner and slip st across to join pieces; finish off.

Afghan Edging

Fold Pocket to the front, matching long edge of Pocket with the seam. With **right** side facing and working through both thicknesses of Pocket, join Yellow with slip st in bottom corner; ch 1, sc in each hdc across Pocket to join; sc in each hdc around the blanket working 3 sc in center hdc of each corner 3-hdc group to the opposite end of the Pocket; working through both thicknesses of Pocket, sc in each hdc across to join; finish off.

LARGE STAR (Make 3)

Rnd 1: With Yellow, ch 4, 11 dc in fourth ch from hook; join with slip st to top of beginning ch-4: 12 sts.

Rnd 2: ★ Ch 5, sc in second ch from hook, hdc in next ch, dc in next ch, tr in last ch, skip next dc, slip st in next dc; repeat from ★ around working last slip st in same st as joining; finish off: 6 points.

SMALL STAR (Make 3)

With Yellow, ch 5; join with slip st to form a ring.

Rnd 1: Ch 1, ★ sc in ring, ch 4, sc in second ch from hook, hdc in next ch, dc in last ch; repeat from ★ 4 times more; join with slip st to first sc, finish off: 5 points.

FINISHING

With Yellow, sew the three Large Stars on Star Section of Body.

Mark the Pocket where you want the separate Pockets to be. With Yellow, sew one Small Star on each Pocket section.

With Yellow, backstitch across Pocket to create three separate pockets *(Fig. 17, page 143)*.

Design by Sheryl Means.

SO CUTE SAFARI TOY

 EASY

Finished Height: Approximately 10½" (26.5 cm)

GAUGE INFORMATION
Gauge is not of great importance as long as your crochet fabric is very dense.

STITCH GUIDE
SINGLE CROCHET 2 TOGETHER
(abbreviated sc2tog)
Pull up a loop in each of next 2 sc, YO and draw through all 3 loops on hook (**counts as one sc**).

STAND
Rnd 1 (Right side): With color indicated, make an adjustable loop to form a ring *(Figs. 3a-d, page 139)*; work 8 sc in ring; do **not** join, place a marker to indicate the beginning of the rnd *(see Markers, page 140)*.

Note: Loop a short piece of yarn around any stitch to mark Rnd 1 as **right** side.

Rnd 2: 2 Sc in each sc around: 16 sc.

Rnd 3: (Sc in next sc, 2 sc in next sc) around: 24 sc.

Rnd 4: (Sc in next 2 sc, 2 sc in next sc) around: 32 sc.

Rnd 5: (Sc in next 3 sc, 2 sc in next sc) around: 40 sc.

Rnd 6: (Sc in next 4 sc, 2 sc in next sc) around: 48 sc.

Rnd 7: (Sc in next 5 sc, 2 sc in next sc) around: 56 sc.

Rnd 8: (Sc in next 6 sc, 2 sc in next sc) around: 64 sc.

Rnd 9: (Sc in next 7 sc, 2 sc in next sc) around: 72 sc.

Rnd 10: (Sc in next 8 sc, 2 sc in next sc) around: 80 sc.

Rnd 11: (Sc in next 9 sc, 2 sc in next sc) around: 88 sc.

Rnd 12: (Sc in next 10 sc, 2 sc in next sc) around: 96 sc.

Rnd 13: Sc in each sc around.

Rnd 14: (Sc in next 11 sc, 2 sc in next sc) around: 104 sc.

Rnd 15: (Sc in next 12 sc, 2 sc in next sc) around: 112 sc.

Rnd 16: (Sc in next 13 sc, 2 sc in next sc) around: 120 sc.

SHOPPING LIST

Yarn
(Medium Weight)
☐ Blue - 150 yards (137 meters)
☐ Green - 40 yards (36.5 meters)
☐ Yellow - 40 yards (36.5 meters)
☐ Orange - 35 yards (32 meters)
☐ Red - 25 yards (23 meters)
☐ White - 15 yards (13.5 meters)

Crochet Hook
☐ Size E (3.5 mm)

Additional Supplies
☐ 9½" (24 cm) Plastic canvas circle
☐ Polyester fiberfill
☐ Yarn needle

SO CUTE SAFARI TOY

Using the crocheted circle as a pattern, trim plastic canvas circle slightly larger than the crocheted piece; set piece aside.

Rnd 17: (Sc in next 13 sc, sc2tog) around: 112 sc.

Rnd 18: (Sc in next 12 sc, sc2tog) around: 104 sc.

Rnd 19: (Sc in next 11 sc, sc2tog) around: 96 sc.

Rnd 20: (Sc in next 10 sc, sc2tog) around: 88 sc.

Insert plastic canvas circle inside crocheted piece to form the bottom of the stand.

Rnd 21: (Sc in next 9 sc, sc2tog) around: 80 sc.

Rnd 22: (Sc in next 8 sc, sc2tog) around: 72 sc.

Rnd 23: (Sc in next 7 sc, sc2tog) around: 64 sc.

Rnd 24: (Sc in next 6 sc, sc2tog) around: 56 sc.

Rnd 25: (Sc in next 5 sc, sc2tog) around: 48 sc.

Rnd 26: (Sc in next 4 sc, sc2tog) around: 40 sc.

Rnd 27: (Sc in next 6 sc, sc2tog) around: 35 sc.

Rnds 28-35: Sc in each sc around.

Stuff piece firmly with polyester fiberfill.

Rnd 36: (Sc in next 5 sc, sc2tog) around: 30 sc.

Rnds 37-44: Sc in each sc around.

Add polyester fiberfill as you continue to work.

Rnd 45: (Sc in next 4 sc, sc2tog) around: 25 sc.

Rnds 46 and 47: Sc in each sc around.

Rnd 48: (Sc in next 3 sc, sc2tog) around: 20 sc.

Rnds 49-54: Sc in each sc around.

Rnd 55: (Sc in next 2 sc, sc2tog) around: 15 sc.

Rnds 56-59: Sc in each sc around.

Rnd 60: Sc2tog around until only 5 sts remain; slip st in next sc, finish off leaving a long end for sewing.

Thread tapestry needle with long end and weave needle through sts on last rnd *(Fig. 15, page 142)*; pull tightly to close and secure end.

RINGS

Ring lengths may need to be adjusted depending on your stitch tension. Looser stitches will stretch more when stuffed so you may need to decrease the number of rounds. You may measure the ring around the stand before finishing and add just the number of rounds as needed.

SO CUTE SAFARI TOY

Elephant Bottom Ring
Rnd 1 (Right side): With Teal, make an adjustable loop to form a ring; work 6 sc in ring; do **not** join, place a marker to indicate the beginning of the rnd.

Rnd 2: 2 Sc in each sc around: 12 sc.

Rnd 3: (Sc in next sc, 2 sc in next sc) around: 18 sc.

Rnd 4: Sc in each sc around.

Repeat Rnd 4 for a total of 70 rnds, stuffing the tube firmly approximately every 10 rnds; slip st in next sc, finish off leaving a long end for sewing.

Sew the tube to itself to form a ring.

HEAD
Rnd 1 (Right side): With Teal, make an adjustable loop to form a ring; work 6 sc in ring; do **not** join, place a marker to indicate the beginning of the rnd.

Note: Mark Rnd 1 as **right** side.

Rnd 2: 2 Sc in each sc around: 12 sc.

Rnd 3: (Sc in next sc, 2 sc in next sc) around: 18 sc.

Rnd 4: (Sc in next 2 sc, 2 sc in next sc) around: 24 sc.

Rnds 5-7: Sc in each sc around.

Rnd 8: (Sc in next 2 sc, sc2tog) around: 18 sc.

Rnd 9: (Sc in next sc, sc2tog) around: 12 sc.

Stuff piece with polyester fiberfill.

Rnd 10: Sc2tog around; slip st in next sc, finish off leaving a long end for sewing.

Sew the Head to the ring at joining so that it sits slightly raised.

FOOT (Make 4)
Rnd 1 (Right side): With Lt Grey, make an adjustable loop to form a ring; work 6 sc in ring; do **not** join, place a marker to indicate the beginning of the rnd.

Note: Mark Rnd 1 as **right** side.

Rnd 2: 2 Sc in each sc around changing to Teal in last sc made *(Fig. 7b, page 140)*; cut Lt Grey: 12 sc.

Rnds 3-6: Sc in each sc around; at end of Rnd 6, slip st in next sc, finish off leaving a long end for sewing.

Sew Feet evenly spaced around ring.

TRUNK
Rnd 1 (Right side): With Lt Grey, make an adjustable loop to form a ring; work 6 sc in ring changing to Teal in last sc made; cut Lt Grey, do **not** join, place a marker to indicate the beginning of the rnd.

Note: Mark Rnd 1 as **right** side.

Rnds 2-5: Sc in each sc around.

Rnd 6: (Sc in next sc, 2 sc in next sc) around: 9 sc.

Rnd 7: (Sc in next 2 sc, 2 sc in next sc) around: 12 sc.

Rnd 8: (Sc in next 3 sc, 2 sc in next sc) around: 15 sc.

Rnd 9: (Sc in next 4 sc, 2 sc in next sc) around: 18 sc.

Rnd 10: Sc in each sc around; slip st in next sc, finish off leaving a long end for sewing.

With long end, stitch down from slip st to tip of Trunk and then back up to edge of Rnd 10. Pull tight to force tip to curl up. Knot yarn to side of trunk to hold curled shape.

EAR (Make 2)
Inner
Rnd 1 (Right side): With Lt Grey, make an adjustable loop to form a ring; work 6 sc in ring; do **not** join, place a marker to indicate the beginning of the rnd.

Note: Mark Rnd 1 as **right** side.

Rnd 2: 2 Sc in each sc around: 12 sc.

Rnd 3: (Sc in next sc, 2 sc in next sc) around; slip st in next sc, finish off leaving a long end for sewing: 18 sts.

Outer
Rnd 1 (Right side): With Teal, make an adjustable loop to form a ring; work 6 sc in ring; do **not** join, place a marker to indicate the beginning of the rnd.

Note: Mark Rnd 1 as right side.

Rnd 2: 2 Sc in each sc around: 12 sc.

Rnd 3: (Sc in next sc, 2 sc in next sc) around: 18 sc.

Rnd 4: (Sc in next 2 sc, 2 sc in next sc) around; slip st in next sc, finish off: 24 sts.

With **wrong** sides together and using long end, sew Inner and Outer Ear together.

TAIL

Holding 2 strands each of Teal and Lt Grey together, ch 4; finish off. Trim strands at one end to ½" (12 mm).

Using photo as a guide for placement:
- Sew Trunk to Head, stuffing lightly.
- Sew Ears to each side of Head
- Sew Tail to back of ring
- With Black embroidery floss, add satin stitch eyes *(Figs. 19a & b, page 143)*.

Hippo Second Ring

With Blue, work same as Elephant Bottom Ring for a total of 60 rnds.

HEAD

With Blue, work same as Elephant Bottom Ring Head, page 55.

FOOT (Make 4)

Work same as Elephant Bottom Ring Foot, using Lt Blue for Rnds 1 and 2 and Blue for the remainder of the Foot.

SNOUT

Rnd 1 (Right side): With Lt Blue, ch 8; sc in second ch from hook and in next 5 chs, 3 sc in last ch; working in free loops on opposite side of ch *(Fig. 6b, page 140)*, sc in next 6 chs, 3 sc in next ch; do **not** join, place a marker to indicate the beginning of the rnd: 18 sc.

Note: Mark Rnd 1 as **right** side.

Rnds 2 and 3: Sc in each sc around; at end of Rnd 3, slip st in next sc, finish off leaving a long end for sewing.

EAR (Make 2)

Rnd 1 (Right side): With Blue, make an adjustable loop to form a ring; work 6 sc in ring; do **not** join, finish off leaving a long end for sewing.

TAIL

With Blue, ch 4; sc in second ch from hook and in last 2 chs; finish off leaving a long end for sewing.

Using photo as a guide for placement:
- Sew Snout to Head, stuffing lightly.
- Sew Ears to each side of Head.
- Sew Tail to back of ring.
- With Black embroidery floss, add satin stitch eyes and straight stitch nostrils *(Fig. 18, page 143)*.
- With White yarn, add a vertical straight stitch tooth at each side of Snout.

Lion Third Ring

With Gold, work same as Elephant Bottom Ring for a total of 50 rnds.

HEAD

With Gold, work same as Elephant Bottom Ring Head.

FOOT (Make 4)

Work same as Elephant Bottom Ring Foot, using Dk Yellow for Rnds 1 and 2 and Gold for the remainder of the Foot.

CHEEK (Make 2)

Rnd 1 (Right side): With Dk Yellow, make an adjustable loop to form a ring; work 6 sc in ring; do **not** join, place a marker to indicate the beginning of the rnd.

Note: Mark Rnd 1 as **right** side.

Rnd 2: 2 Sc in each sc around; slip st in next sc, finish off leaving a long end for sewing.

EAR (Make 2)

Row 1 (Right side): With Dk Yellow, ch 4; sc in second ch from hook and in last 2 chs: 3 sc.

Note: Mark Row 1 as **right** side.

Row 2: Turn; skip first sc, sc in last 2 sc: 2 sc.

Row 3: Turn; skip first sc, slip st in last sc; finish off leaving long end for sewing.

SO CUTE SAFARI TOY

MANE
With Orange, ch 25; sc in second ch from hook, 3 dc in next ch, (sc in next ch, 3 dc in next ch) across; finish off leaving a long end for sewing.

TAIL
Holding 2 strands each of Gold and Dk Yellow together, ch 4; finish off. Trim strands at one end to ½" (12 mm).

Using photo as a guide for placement:
- Sew Cheeks to Head, stuffing lightly.
- Sew Ears to top of Head.
- Sew Mane around Head (in front of Ears).
- Sew Tail to back of ring.
- With Black embroidery floss, add satin stitch nose, a straight stitch vertical line between Cheeks, and straight stitch eyes.
- With White embroidery floss, add straight stitch whiskers.

Monkey Top Ring
With Dk Brown, work same as Elephant Bottom Ring for a total of 40 rnds.

HEAD
With Dk Brown, work same as Elephant Bottom Ring Head.

FOOT (Make 4)
Work same as Elephant Bottom Ring Foot, using Tan for Rnds 1 and 2 and Dk Brown for remainder of Foot.

FACE
Rnd 1 (Right side): With Tan, make an adjustable loop to form a ring; work 6 sc in ring; do **not** join, place a marker to indicated the beginning of the rnd.

Note: Mark Rnd 1 as **right** side.

Rnd 2: 2 Sc in each sc around: 12 sc.

Rnd 3: (Sc in next sc, 2 sc in next sc) around; slip st in next sc, finish off leaving a long end for sewing: 18 sts.

SNOUT
Rnd 1 (Right side): With Tan, ch 6; sc in second ch from hook and in next 3 chs, 3 sc in last ch; working in free loops on opposite side of ch, sc in next 4 chs, 3 sc in next ch; do **not** join, place a marker to indicate the beginning of the rnd: 14 sc.

Note: Mark Rnd 1 as **right** side.

Rnd 2: Sc in each sc around; slip st in next sc, finish off leaving a long end for sewing.

EAR (Make 2)
Rnd 1 (Right side): With Dk Brown, make an adjustable loop to form a ring; work 8 sc in ring; join with slip st to first sc, finish off leaving a long end for sewing.

TAIL
With Dk Brown, ch 18; sc in second ch from hook and in each ch across; finish off leaving a long end for sewing.

Using photo as a guide for placement:
- Sew Face to Head.
- Sew Snout to Head, stuffing lightly.
- Sew Ears to each side of Head.
- Sew Tail to back of ring.
- With Black embroidery floss, add satin stitch eyes and straight stitch nostrils and a mouth.

Design by Tamara Ramsey.

SKIRT DIAPER COVER

 EASY

SIZE INFORMATION
Finished Measurements:

Size	Waist	Rise (from top of front to top of back)
0-3 Months	12½" (32 cm)	13" (33 cm)
3-6 Months	13¾" (35 cm)	15" (38 cm)
6-12 Months	15" (38 cm)	16½" (42 cm)

Size Note: We have printed the instructions for the sizes in different colors to make it easier for you to find:
- Size 0-3 months in Blue
- Size 3-6 months in Pink
- Size 6-12 months in Green

Instructions in Black apply to all sizes.

GAUGE INFORMATION
14 sc and 16 rows = 4" (10 cm)
    14 dc and 8 rows = 4" (10 cm)
Gauge Swatch: 4" (10 cm) square
With Blue, ch 15.
Row 1: Sc in second ch from hook and in each ch across: 14 sc.
Rows 2-16: Ch 1, turn; sc in each sc across.
Finish off.

STITCH GUIDE
SINGLE CROCHET 2 TOGETHER
    (abbreviated sc2tog)
Pull up a loop in each of next 2 sts, YO and draw through all 3 loops on hook **(counts as one sc)**.

BODY
With Blue and leaving a long end for sewing, ch 23{25-27}.

Row 1 (Right side): Sc in second ch from hook and in each ch across: 22{24-26} sc.

Note: Loop a short piece of yarn around any stitch to mark Row 1 as **right** side.

Row 2: Ch 1, turn; sc in each sc across.

Row 3: Ch 1, turn; sc in Back Loop Only of each sc across *(Fig. 5, page 140)*.

Rows 4 thru 9{10-11}: Ch 2 **(does not count as a st, now and throughout)**, turn; dc in both loops of each st across.

SHOPPING LIST

Yarn
(Medium Weight) 4
[5 ounces, 251 yards
(142 grams, 230 meters)
per skein]:
☐ Blue - 1 skein
☐ Pink - 1 skein

Crochet Hook
☐ Size J (6 mm)
    or size needed for gauge

Additional Supplies
☐ Yarn needle

SKIRT DIAPER COVER

Rows 10{11-12} thru 14{15-16} (Decrease rows)**:** Ch 1, turn; sc in first st, sc2tog, sc in each st across to last 3 sts, sc2tog, sc in last st: 12{14-16} sc.

Rows 15{16-17} thru 26{31-34}: Ch 1, turn; sc in each sc across.

Rows 27{32-35} thru 31{36-39} (Increase rows)**:** Ch 1, turn; 2 sc in first sc, sc in each sc across to last sc, 2 sc in last sc: 22{24-26} sc.

Rows 32{37-40} thru 37{43-47}: Ch 2, turn; dc in each st across.

Row 38{44-48}: Ch 1, turn; sc in each dc across.

Row 39{45-49}: Ch 1, turn; sc in Back Loop Only of each sc across.

Row 40{46-50}: Ch 1, turn; sc in both loops of each sc across; finish off leaving a long end for sewing.

Using long end and matching rows, use mattress stitch *(Figs. 14a & b, page 142)* to join first and last 9{10-11} rows together on each side.

LEG EDGING

Rnd 1: With **right** side facing, join Blue with sc at seam on Leg opening *(see joining With Sc, page 138)*; sc evenly around; join with slip st to first sc.

Rnd 2: Ch 1, sc in each sc around; join with slip st to first sc, finish off.

Repeat for second Leg.

SKIRT

Rnd 1: With **right** side facing, holding waist down, and working in free loops of sc on Row 2 and Row 38{44-48} *(Fig. 6a, page 140)*, join Pink with sc in first sc; sc in each st around increasing 8 sc evenly spaced; join with slip st to first sc: 52{56-60} sc.

Rnd 2: Ch 3 **(counts as first dc, now and throughout)**, dc in next sc, ch 2, skip next 2 sc, ★ dc in next 2 sc, ch 2, skip next 2 sc; repeat from ★ around; join with slip st to first dc: 26{28-30} dc and 13{14-15} ch-2 sps.

Rnd 3: Ch 1, sc in first 2 dc, ch 2, skip next ch-2 sp, ★ sc in next 2 dc, ch 2, skip next ch-2 sp; repeat from ★ around; join with slip st to first sc.

Rnd 4: Ch 3, dc in next sc, ch 2, skip next ch-2 sp, ★ dc in next 2 sc, ch 2, skip next ch-2 sp; repeat from ★ around; join with slip st to first dc.

Rnds 5 thru 10{10-12}: Repeat Rnds 3 and 4, 3{3-4} times.

Rnd 11{11-13}: Slip st in next dc, 5 dc in next ch-2 sp, ★ skip next dc, slip st in next dc, 5 dc in next ch-2 sp; repeat from ★ around; join with slip st to first slip st, finish off.

Design by Kristi Simpson.

STAR BRIGHT TOY

 EASY

Finished Size: Approximately 12" (30.5 cm) from tip to tip

GAUGE INFORMATION
Gauge is not important, but the stitches should be close enough together so that the fiberfill stuffing does not show.

STITCH GUIDE
SINGLE CROCHET 2 STITCHES TOGETHER *(abbreviated sc2tog)*
Pull up a loop in each of next 2 sts, YO and draw through all 3 loops on hook (**counts as one sc**).

STAR (Make 2)
Circle
Rnd 1 (Right side): With Yellow, make an adjustable ring *(Figs. 3a-d, page 139)*; ch 1, work 10 sc in ring; join with slip st to first sc.

Note: Loop a short piece of yarn around any stitch to mark Rnd 1 as **right** side.

Rnd 2: Ch 1, 2 sc in same st as joining and in each sc around; join with slip st to first sc: 20 sc.

Rnd 3: Ch 1, sc in same st as joining, 2 sc in next sc, (sc in next sc, 2 sc in next sc) around; join with slip st to first sc: 30 sc.

Rnd 4: Ch 1, sc in same st as joining and in next sc, 2 sc in next sc, (sc in next 2 sc, 2 sc in next sc) around; join with slip st to first sc: 40 sc.

Rnd 5: Ch 1, sc in same st as joining and in next 2 sc, 2 sc in next sc, (sc in next 3 sc, 2 sc in next sc) around; join with slip st to first sc: 50 sc.

Rnd 6: Ch 1, sc in same st as joining and in next 3 sc, 2 sc in next sc, (sc in next 4 sc, 2 sc in next sc) around; join with slip st to first sc: 60 sc.

Rnds 7-10: Ch 1, sc in same st as joining and in each sc around; join with slip st to first sc; do **not** finish off.

SHOPPING LIST

Yarn
(Medium Weight) [4]
[3.5 ounces, 170 yards (100 grams, 156 meters) per skein]:
☐ Yellow - 1 skein
☐ Black or Navy - small amount for face

Crochet Hook
☐ Size H (5 mm)

Additional Supplies
☐ Yarn needle
☐ Washable polyester fiberfill

First Ray

Row 1: Ch 1, sc in same st as joining and in next 11 sc, leave remaining sc unworked: 12 sc.

Row 2: Ch 1, turn; sc in each sc across.

Row 3 (Decrease row): Ch 1, turn; beginning in first sc, sc2tog, sc in each sc across to last 2 sc, sc2tog: 10 sc.

Rows 4-6: Ch 1, turn; sc in each sc across.

Rows 7-10: Repeat Rows 3-6: 8 sc.

Row 11 (Decrease row): Ch 1, turn; beginning in first sc, sc2tog, sc in each sc across to last 2 sc, sc2tog: 6 sc.

Row 12: Ch 1, turn; sc in each sc across.

Rows 13 and 14: Repeat Rows 11 and 12: 4 sc.

Row 15: Ch 1, turn; beginning in first sc, sc2tog twice: 2 sc.

Row 16: Ch 1, turn; sc in both sc; finish off.

Next 4 Rays

With **right** side facing, join Yellow with slip st in next sc on Rnd 10 of Circle.

Repeat Rows 1-16 of First Ray; at end of fifth Ray, do **not** finish off.

Edging

Ch 1, sc evenly around Star, working one sc between each Ray; join with slip st to first sc, finish off.

FINISHING

Using Face Diagrams and photos as a guide for placement, embroider a face on each side of Star using Black or Navy *(see Embroidery Stitches, page 143)*.

Joining

Hold **wrong** side of Stars together with awake side facing. Working through both thicknesses, join Yellow with slip st in any sc; ch 1, sc in each sc around 3 Rays. Stuff Star with fiberfill. Sc in each sc around remaining 2 Rays adding additional fiberfill as needed; join with slip st to first sc, finish off.

Design by Sheryl Means.

Face Diagrams

PRETZEL RATTLE

 EASY

Finished Size: 8" wide x 6" high (20.5 cm x 15 cm) pretzel shaped

GAUGE INFORMATION
Gauge Swatch: 1¼" (3 cm) diameter
Work same as Body through Rnd 3: 18 sc.

STITCH GUIDE
SINGLE CROCHET 2 TOGETHER *(abbreviated sc2tog)*
Pull up a loop in each of next 2 sc, YO and draw through all 3 loops on hook **(counts as one sc)**.

PREPARE RATTLE
Cover the unopened tube of beads with clear, waterproof packing tape, making sure the lid is secure and the entire tube is completely covered. *Note:* Rattle may be omitted for extra safety.

COLOR SEQUENCE
Work 18 rnds **each** of Blue, Green, Red, Lt Navy, Orange, Pink, Yellow, and 16 rnds of Coral.

BODY
Rnd 1 (Right side)**:** With Blue and leaving a long end for sewing, ch 2; 6 sc in second ch from hook; do **not** join, place marker to mark beginning of rnd *(see Markers, page 140)*.

Rnd 2: 2 Sc in each sc around: 12 sc.

Rnd 3: (Sc in next sc, 2 sc in next sc) around: 18 sc.

Rnd 4: Sc in each sc around.

Thread yarn needle with beginning long end, weave needle through sts on Rnd 1 *(Fig. 15, page 142)*, pull tightly to close and secure end.

Repeat Rnd 4 for 14 rnds **more or** until at least a 10" (25.5 cm) length of yarn remains, ending at marker and changing to Green in last sc made *(Fig. 7a, page 140)*.

Secure both Blue and Green yarn ends, cut Blue and set remaining length aside to use later.

SHOPPING LIST

Yarn
(Medium Weight) [MEDIUM 4]
[0.35 ounce, 17 yards (10 grams, 16 meters) per skein]:
☐ Blue - 1 skein
☐ Green - 1 skein
☐ Red - 1 skein
☐ Lt Navy - 1 skein
☐ Orange - 1 skein
☐ Pink - 1 skein
☐ Yellow - 1 skein
☐ Coral - 1 skein

Crochet Hook
☐ Size 7 (4.5 mm)
 or size needed for gauge

Additional Supplies
☐ Unopened plastic tube of beads [3" long x 2" circumference (7.5 cm x 5 cm)]
☐ Clear, waterproof packing tape
☐ Polyester fiberfill
☐ Yarn needle

Stuff 1" (2.5 cm) of the piece with fiberfill, insert rattle into the center; then add more fiberfill around the rattle.

Continue adding fiberfill as you work the entire piece.

Repeat Rnd 4 following the color sequence; do **not** cut last color.

Next Rnd: (Sc in next sc, sc2tog) around: 12 sc.

Last Rnd: Sc2tog around; finish off leaving a long end for sewing: 6 sc.

Thread yarn needle with long end, weave needle through sts on last rnd, pull tightly to close and secure end.

Form piece into a pretzel shape. With matching colors, sew pretzel together at center cross; then secure each end in place.

Design by Sharon H. Silverman.

IRISH LUCK BLANKET

 EASY

Finished Size: 32½" x 38" (82.5 cm x 96.5 cm)

GAUGE INFORMATION
14 hdc and 9 rows = 4" (10 cm)
Gauge Swatch: 4" (10 cm) square
Ch 15.
Row 1: Hdc in third ch from hook **(2 skipped chs count as first hdc)** and in each ch across: 14 hdc.
Rows 2-9: Ch 2 **(counts as first hdc)**, turn; hdc in next hdc and in each hdc across.
Finish off.

STITCH GUIDE
BACK POST DOUBLE CROCHET (abbreviated BPdc)
YO, insert hook from **back** to **front** around post of st indicated *(Fig. 10, page 141)*, YO and pull up a loop (3 loops on hook), (YO and draw through 2 loops on hook) twice.

FRONT POST DOUBLE CROCHET (abbreviated FPdc)
YO, insert hook from **front** to **back** around post of st indicated *(Fig. 10, page 141)*, YO and pull up a loop (3 loops on hook), (YO and draw through 2 loops on hook) twice.

FRONT POST TREBLE CROCHET (abbreviated FPtr)
YO twice, insert hook from **front** to **back** around post of st indicated *(Fig. 10, page 141)*, YO and pull up a loop even with loops on hook (4 loops on hook), (YO and draw through 2 loops on hook) 3 times.
Skip hdc **behind** FPtr.

FRONT POST DOUBLE TREBLE CROCHET (abbreviated FPdtr)
YO 3 times, insert hook from **front** to **back** around post of st indicated *(Fig. 10, page 141)*, YO and pull up a loop even with loops on hook (5 loops on hook), (YO and draw through 2 loops on hook) 4 times.
Skip hdc **behind** FPdtr.

POPCORN (uses one hdc)
5 Dc in hdc indicated, drop loop from hook, insert hook in first dc of 5-dc group, hook dropped loop and draw through dc.

SHOPPING LIST

Yarn
(Light Weight)
[3.5 ounces, 254 yards
(100 grams, 232 meters)
per skein]:
☐ 6 skeins

Crochet Hook
☐ Size I (5.5 mm)
 or size needed for gauge

Additional Supplies
☐ Tapestry needle

67

IRISH LUCK BLANKET

DIAMOND PANEL

Finished Size:
10½" wide x 35½" long
(26.5 cm x 90 cm)

Ch 36.

Row 1 (Right side): Hdc in third ch from hook (**2 skipped chs count as first hdc**) and in each ch across: 35 hdc.

Note: Loop a short piece of yarn around any stitch to mark Row 1 as **right** side **and** bottom edge.

Row 2: Ch 2 (**counts as first hdc, now and throughout**), turn; hdc in next hdc and in each hdc across.

Row 3: Ch 2, turn; hdc in next 2 hdc, work FPtr around each of next 2 hdc 2 rows **below**, hdc in next 10 hdc, skip next 3 hdc 2 rows **below**, work FPdtr around each of next 2 hdc 2 rows **below**, hdc in next hdc, working in **front** of last 2 FPdtr made, work FPdtr around each of first 2 skipped hdc 2 rows **below**, hdc in next 10 hdc, work FPtr around each of next 2 hdc 2 rows **below**, hdc in last 3 hdc.

Row 4: Ch 2, turn; hdc in next st and in each st across.

Row 5: Ch 2, turn; hdc in next 2 hdc, work FPtr around each of next 2 FPtr 2 rows **below**, hdc in next 8 hdc, work FPdtr around each of next 2 FPdtr 2 rows **below**, hdc in next 5 hdc, work FPdtr around each of next 2 FPdtr 2 rows **below**, hdc in next 8 hdc, work FPtr around each of next 2 FPtr 2 rows **below**, hdc in last 3 hdc.

Row 6: Ch 2, turn; hdc in next st and in each st across.

Row 7: Ch 2, turn; hdc in next 2 hdc, work FPtr around each of next 2 FPtr 2 rows **below**, hdc in next 6 hdc, work FPdtr around each of next 2 FPdtr 2 rows **below**, hdc in next 9 hdc, work FPdtr around each of next 2 FPdtr 2 rows **below**, hdc in next 6 hdc, work FPtr around each of next 2 FPtr 2 rows **below**, hdc in last 3 hdc.

Row 8: Ch 2, turn; hdc in next st and in each st across.

Row 9: Ch 2, turn; hdc in next 2 hdc, work FPtr around each of next 2 FPtr 2 rows **below**, hdc in next 4 hdc, work FPdtr around each of next 2 FPdtr 2 rows **below**, hdc in next 13 hdc, work FPdtr around each of next 2 FPdtr 2 rows **below**, hdc in next 4 hdc, work FPtr around each of next 2 FPtr 2 rows **below**, hdc in last 3 hdc.

Row 10: Ch 2, turn; hdc in next st and in each st across.

Row 11: Ch 2, turn; hdc in next 2 hdc, work FPtr around each of next 2 FPtr 2 rows **below**, hdc in next 2 hdc, work FPdtr around each of next 2 FPdtr 2 rows **below**, hdc in next 17 hdc, work FPdtr around each of next 2 FPdtr 2 rows **below**, hdc in next 2 hdc, work FPtr around each of next 2 FPtr 2 rows **below**, hdc in last 3 hdc.

Row 12: Ch 2, turn; hdc in next st and in each st across.

Row 13: Ch 2, turn; (hdc in next 2 hdc, work FPtr around each of next 2 FPsts 2 rows **below**) twice, hdc in next 8 hdc, work Popcorn in next hdc, hdc in next 8 hdc, work FPtr around each of next 2 FPdtr 2 rows **below**, hdc in next 2 hdc, work FPtr around each of next 2 FPtr 2 rows **below**, hdc in last 3 hdc.

Row 14: Ch 2, turn; hdc in next st and in each st across.

Row 15: Ch 2, turn; hdc in next 2 hdc, work FPtr around each of next 2 FPtr 2 rows **below**, hdc in next 4 hdc, work FPdtr around each of next 2 FPtr 2 rows **below**, hdc in next 13 hdc, work FPdtr around each of next 2 FPtr 2 rows **below**, hdc in next 4 hdc, work FPtr around each of next 2 FPtr 2 rows below, hdc in last 3 hdc.

Row 16: Ch 2, turn; hdc in next st and in each st across.

Row 17: Ch 2, turn; hdc in next 2 hdc, work FPtr around each of next 2 FPtr 2 rows **below**, hdc in next 6 hdc, work FPdtr around each of next 2 FPdtr 2 rows **below**, hdc in next 9 hdc, work FPdtr around each of next 2 FPdtr 2 rows **below**, hdc in next 6 hdc, work FPtr around each of next 2 FPtr 2 rows **below**, hdc in last 3 hdc.

Row 18: Ch 2, turn; hdc in next st and in each st across.

Row 19: Ch 2, turn; hdc in next 2 hdc, work FPtr around each of next 2 FPtr 2 rows **below**, hdc in next 8 hdc, work FPdtr around each of next 2 FPdtr 2 rows **below**, hdc in next 5 hdc, work FPdtr around each of next 2 FPdtr 2 rows **below**, hdc in next 8 hdc, work FPtr around each of next 2 FPtr 2 rows **below**, hdc in last 3 hdc.

Row 20: Ch 2, turn; hdc in next st and in each st across.

Row 21: Ch 2, turn; hdc in next 2 hdc, work FPtr around each of next 2 FPtr 2 rows **below**, hdc in next 10 hdc, work FPdtr around each of next 2 FPdtr 2 rows **below**, hdc in next hdc, work FPdtr around each of next 2 FPdtr 2 rows **below**, hdc in next 10 hdc, work FPtr around each of next 2 FPtr 2 rows **below**, hdc in last 3 hdc.

Row 22: Ch 2, turn; hdc in next st and in each st across.

Row 23: Ch 2, turn; hdc in next 2 hdc, work FPtr around each of next 2 FPtr 2 rows **below**, hdc in next 10 hdc, skip next 2 FPdtr 2 rows **below**, work FPdtr around each of next 2 FPdtr 2 rows **below**, hdc in next hdc, working in **front** of last 2 FPdtr made, work FPdtr around each of 2 skipped FPdtr 2 rows **below**, hdc in next 10 hdc, work FPtr around each of next 2 FPtr 2 rows **below**, hdc in last 3 hdc.

Row 24: Ch 2, turn; hdc in next st and in each st across.

Rows 25-84: Repeat Rows 5-24, 3 times.

Finish off.

BASKETWEAVE PANEL
(Make 2)
Finished Size: 9¾" wide x 35½" long (25 cm x 90 cm)

Ch 40.

Row 1 (Right side)**:** Dc in fourth ch from hook (**3 skipped chs count as first dc**) and in each ch across: 38 dc.

Note: Mark Row 1 as **right** side **and** bottom edge.

Row 2: Ch 2, turn; work BPdc around each of next 4 dc, ★ work FPdc around each of next 4 dc, work BPdc around each of next 4 dc; repeat from ★ across to last dc, hdc in last dc.

Rows 3 and 4: Ch 2, turn; work FPdc around each of next 4 sts, ★ work BPdc around each of next 4 sts, work FPdc around each of next 4 sts; repeat from ★ across to last hdc, hdc in last hdc.

Rows 5 and 6: Ch 2, turn; work BPdc around each of next 4 sts, ★ work FPdc around each of next 4 sts, work BPdc around each of next 4 sts; repeat from ★ across to last hdc, hdc in last hdc.

Repeat Rows 3-6 for pattern until piece measures same as Diamond Panel, ending by working Row 3.

Finish off.

ASSEMBLY
With bottom edges at the same end and placing Diamond Panel in the center, sew Panels together.

EDGING
Rnd 1: With **right** side facing, join yarn with slip st in any corner; ch 1, ★ 3 sc in corner, work an odd number of sc across to next corner; repeat from ★ around; join with slip st to first sc.

Rnd 2: Slip st in next sc, ch 4 (**counts as first dc plus ch 1**), (dc in same st, ch 1) twice, skip next sc, ★ (dc in next sc, ch 1, skip next sc) across to center sc of next corner, (dc, ch 1) 3 times in center sc, skip next sc; repeat from ★ 2 times **more**, (dc in next sc, ch 1, skip next st) across; join with slip st to first dc.

Rnd 3: Slip st in next ch-1 sp, ch 1, (sc, ch 3, slip st in third ch from hook, sc) in same ch-1 sp and in each ch-1 sp around; join with slip st to first sc, finish off.

Design by Melissa Leapman.

LEXXI DRESS

 EASY

Size: 12 to 18 months

GAUGE INFORMATION
In Body pattern,
    (sc, dc) 9 times and 16 rows/rnds = 4" (10 cm)
In Skirt pattern,
    3 repeats (15 sts and 3 ch-2 sps) and 8 rnds = 3¼" (8.25 cm)

Gauge Swatch: 4" (10 cm) square
With Black, ch 19.
Row 1 (Right side): Sc in second ch from hook, dc in next ch, (sc in next ch, dc in next ch) across: 18 sts.
Rows 2-16: Ch 1, turn; sc in first dc, dc in next sc, (sc in next dc, dc in next sc) across.
Finish off.

STITCH GUIDE
TREBLE CROCHET *(abbreviated tr)*
YO twice, insert hook in sc indicated, YO and pull up a loop (4 loops on hook), (YO and draw through 2 loops on hook) 3 times.

SINGLE CROCHET 2 TOGETHER
    (abbreviated sc2tog)
Pull up a loop in each of next 2 sts, YO and draw through all 3 loops on hook (counts as one sc).

DOUBLE CROCHET 2 TOGETHER
    (abbreviated dc2tog) (uses next 2 sts)
★ YO, insert hook in next st, YO and pull up a loop, YO and draw through 2 loops on hook; repeat from ★ once more, YO and draw through all 3 loops on hook (counts as one dc).

BODY
With Black, ch 84 loosely; being careful **not** to twist ch, join with slip st to form a ring.

Rnd 1 (Right side): Ch 1, sc in same st as joining, dc in next ch, (sc in next ch, dc in next ch) around; join with slip st to first sc: 84 sts.

Note: Loop a short piece of yarn around any stitch to mark Rnd 1 as **right** side.

Rnd 2: Ch 3 **(counts as first dc, now and throughout)**, turn; sc in next dc, (dc in next sc, sc in next dc) around; join with slip st to first dc.

SHOPPING LIST

Yarn (Light Weight) [3]
[1.75 ounces, 136 yards (50 grams, 125 meters) per skein]:
☐ Black - 3 skeins
☐ White - 1 skein
☐ Red - 10 yards (9 meters)

Crochet Hook
☐ Size G (4 mm)
    or size needed for gauge

Additional Supplies
☐ Tapestry needle

Rnd 3: Ch 1, turn; sc in same st as joining, dc in next sc, (sc in next dc, dc in next sc) around; join with slip st to first sc.

Repeat Rnds 2 and 3 for pattern until Body measures approximately 7½" (19 cm) from beginning ch, ending by working Rnd 2.

Front
ARMHOLE SHAPING
Row 1: Turn; slip st in next 2 sts, [ch 2, dc in next sc **(counts as first dc2tog, now and throughout)**], (sc in next dc, dc in next sc) 17 times, sc2tog, leave remaining 44 sts unworked: 36 sts.

Row 2: Ch 1, turn; beginning in first sc, sc2tog, (dc in next sc, sc in next dc) across to last 2 sts, dc2tog: 34 sts.

Row 3: Ch 2, turn; dc in next sc, (sc in next dc, dc in next sc) across to last 2 sts, sc2tog: 32 sts.

Row 4: Ch 3, turn; sc in next dc, (dc in next sc, sc in next dc) across.

Repeat Row 4 until Armholes measure approximately 1¾" (4.5 cm), ending by working a wrong side row.

NECK SHAPING
First Side

Row 1: Ch 3, turn; (sc in next dc, dc in next sc) 5 times, sc2tog, leave remaining 19 sts unworked: 12 sts.

Row 2: Ch 1, turn; beginning in first sc, sc2tog, (dc in next sc, sc in next dc) across: 11 sts.

Row 3: Ch 3, turn; (sc in next dc, dc in next sc) across to last 2 sts, sc2tog: 10 sts.

Row 4: Ch 1, turn; beginning in first sc, sc2tog, (dc in next sc, sc in next dc) across: 9 sts.

Row 5: Ch 3, turn; (sc in next dc, dc in next sc) across.

Row 6: Ch 1, turn; sc in first dc, (dc in next sc, sc in next dc) across.

LEXXI DRESS

Repeat Rows 5 and 6 until Armholes measure approximately 4" (10 cm), ending by working a **wrong** side row.

Finish off.

Second Side

Row 1: With **right** side facing, skip next 6 sts from First Side and join Black with slip st in next dc; ch 2, (dc in next sc, sc in next dc) across: 12 sts.

Row 2: Ch 3, turn; sc in next dc, (dc in next sc, sc in next dc) across to last 2 sts, dc2tog: 11 sts.

Row 3: Ch 2, turn; (dc in next sc, sc in next dc) across: 10 sts.

Row 4: Ch 3, turn; sc in next dc, (dc in next sc, sc in next dc) across to last 2 sts, dc2tog: 9 sts.

Row 5: Ch 1, turn; sc in first dc, (dc in next sc, sc in next dc) across.

Row 6: Ch 3, turn; (sc in next dc, dc in next sc) across.

Repeat Rows 5 and 6 until Armholes measure approximately 4" (10 cm), ending by working a wrong side row.

Finish off.

Back
ARMHOLE SHAPING

Row 1: With **right** side facing, skip next 4 sts from Front and join Black with slip st in next dc; ch 2, dc in next sc, (sc in next dc, dc in next sc) 17 times, sc2tog, leave remaining sts unworked: 36 sts.

Complete same as Front, leaving long ends for sewing.

With **wrong** sides together and using long ends, working through **both** loops of sts on **both** pieces, whipstitch shoulder seams *(Fig. 13a, page 142)*.

ARMHOLE TRIM

With **right** side facing, join Black with sc in third unworked st at either armhole; sc evenly around; join with slip st to first sc, finish off.

Repeat for second Armhole.

NECK TRIM

With **right** side facing, join Black with sc in sc at center Back; sc evenly around; join with slip st to first sc, finish off.

SKIRT

Rnd 1: With **right** side facing and working in free loops of beginning ch *(Fig. 6b, page 140)*, join White with sc in same st as joining *(see Joining With Sc, page 138)*; sc in each ch around; join with slip st to first sc: 84 sc.

Rnds 2-9: Ch 1, turn; sc in same st as joining and in each sc around; join with slip st to first sc.

Rnd 10: Ch 3, do not turn; dc in same st as joining, skip next sc, (dc, ch 2, dc) in next sc, skip next sc, ★ 3 dc in next sc, skip next sc, (dc, ch 2, dc) in next sc, skip next sc; repeat from ★ around, dc in same st as first dc; join with slip st to first dc: 105 dc and 21 ch-2 sps.

Rnds 11-17: Ch 3, dc in same st as joining, skip next 2 dc, (dc, ch 2, dc) in next ch-2 sp, skip next 2 dc, ★ 3 dc in next dc, skip next 2 dc, (dc, ch 2, dc) in next ch-2 sp, skip next 2 dc; repeat from ★ around, dc in same st as first dc; join with slip st to first dc.

Finish off.

FLOWER

Rnd 1 (Right side): With Red and leaving a long end for sewing, ch 2, 6 sc in second ch from hook; join with slip st to first sc.

Rnd 2: Ch 1, (sc, tr) in same st as joining and in each sc around; join with slip st to first sc: 12 sts.

Rnd 3: Ch 2, skip next tr, ★ slip st in next sc, ch 2, skip next tr; repeat from ★ around; join with slip st to joining slip st: 6 ch-2 sps.

Rnd 4: (Slip st, ch 1, sc, hdc, 3 dc, hdc, sc) in first ch-2 sp **(petal made)**, (sc, hdc, 3 dc, hdc, sc) in next ch-2 sp and in each ch-2 sp around; join with slip st to first sc: 6 petals.

Rnd 5: Slip st in each st around; join with slip st to joining slip st, finish off.

Using photo as a guide for placement and long end, sew Flower to Dress.

Design by Lois J. Long

PUPPY LOVIE

 EASY

Finished Size: Blanket = 13½" (34.5 cm)

GAUGE INFORMATION
In Blanket pattern,
   (3 dc, ch 2) 3 times = 4" (10 cm);
   4 rnds = 2¾" (7 cm)
Gauge Swatch: 3¼" (8.25 cm) square
Work Blanket through Rnd 2: 24 dc and 8 sps.

STITCH GUIDE
SINGLE CROCHET 2 TOGETHER
(abbreviated sc2tog)
Pull up a loop in each of next 2 sts, YO and draw through all 3 loops on hook (**counts as one sc**).

BLANKET
Note: Use larger size hook for entire Blanket.

With larger size hook and Variegated, ch 4; join with slip st to form a ring.

Rnd 1 (Right side): Ch 3 (**counts as first dc, now and throughout**), 2 dc in ring, ch 3, (3 dc in ring, ch 3) 3 times; join with slip st to first dc: 12 dc and 4 ch-3 sps.

Note: Loop a short piece of yarn around any stitch to mark Rnd 1 as **right** side.

Rnd 2: Slip st in next 2 dc and in next ch-3 sp, ch 3, (2 dc, ch 3, 3 dc) in same sp (**corner made**), ch 2, ★ (3 dc, ch 3, 3 dc) in next ch-3 sp (**corner made**), ch 2; repeat from ★ 2 times **more**; join with slip st to first dc: 24 dc and 8 sps.

Rnd 3: Slip st in next 2 dc and in next corner ch-3 sp, ch 3, (2 dc, ch 3, 3 dc) in same corner sp, ch 2, 3 dc in next ch-2 sp, ch 2, ★ (3 dc, ch 3, 3 dc) in next corner ch-3 sp, ch 2, 3 dc in next ch-2 sp, ch 2; repeat from ★ 2 times **more**; join with slip st to first dc, finish off: 36 dc and 12 sps.

SHOPPING LIST

Yarn
(Medium Weight) [4]
[7 ounces, 370 yards
(198 grams, 338 meters) per skein]:
☐ Tan - 1 skein
[5 ounces, 236 yards
(141 grams, 215 meters) per skein]:
☐ Variegated - 1 skein
[3.5 ounces, 190 yards
(100 grams, 174 meters) per skein]:
☐ Brown - 1 skein
☐ Black - small amount

Crochet Hooks
☐ Size F (3.75 mm) (for Head, Eye Patch, Ears & Arms) **and**
☐ Size J (6 mm) (for Blanket)
   or sizes needed for gauge

Additional Supplies
☐ Polyester fiberfill
☐ Yarn needle

Rnd 4: With **right** side facing, join Tan with dc in any corner ch-3 sp *(see Joining With Dc, page 139)*; (2 dc, ch 3, 3 dc) in same corner sp, ch 2, ★ (3 dc in next ch-2 sp, ch 2) across to next corner ch-3 sp, (3 dc, ch 3, 3 dc) in corner sp, ch 2; repeat from ★ 2 times **more**, (3 dc in next ch-2 sp, ch 2) across; join with slip st to first dc: 48 dc and 16 sps.

Rnd 5: Slip st in next 2 dc and in next corner ch-3 sp, ch 3, (2 dc, ch 3, 3 dc) in same corner sp, ch 2, ★ (3 dc in next ch-2 sp, ch 2) across to next corner ch-3 sp, (3 dc, ch 3, 3 dc) in corner sp, ch 2; repeat from ★ 2 times **more**, (3 dc in next ch-2 sp, ch 2) across; join with slip st to first dc, finish off: 60 dc and 20 sps.

Rnd 6: With **right** side facing, join Variegated with dc in any corner ch-3 sp; (2 dc, ch 3, 3 dc) in same corner sp, ch 2, ★ (3 dc in next ch-2 sp, ch 2) across to next corner ch-3 sp, (3 dc, ch 3, 3 dc) in corner sp, ch 2; repeat from ★ 2 times **more**, (3 dc in next ch-2 sp, ch 2) across; join with slip st to first dc: 72 dc and 24 sps.

Rnds 7 and 8: Slip st in next 2 dc and in next corner ch-3 sp, ch 3, (2 dc, ch 3, 3 dc) in same corner sp, ch 2, ★ (3 dc in next ch-2 sp, ch 2) across to next corner ch-3 sp, (3 dc, ch 3, 3 dc) in corner sp, ch 2; repeat from ★ 2 times **more**, (3 dc in next ch-2 sp, ch 2) across; join with slip st to first dc: 96 dc and 32 sps.

Finish off.

Rnds 9 and 10: Repeat Rnds 4 and 5: 120 dc and 40 sps.

HEAD

Rnd 1 (Right side): With Tan, using smaller size hook and an adjustable loop *(Figs. 3a-d, page 139)*, ch 1, 6 sc in ring, pull tail to close ring; place marker to mark beginning of the rnd *(see Markers, page 140)*.

Note: Mark Rnd 1 as **right** side.

Rnd 2: 2 Sc in each sc around: 12 sc.

Rnd 3: (2 Sc in next sc, sc in next sc) around: 18 sc.

Rnd 4: (2 Sc in next sc, sc in next 2 sc) around: 24 sc.

Rnd 5: (2 Sc in next sc, sc in next 3 sc) around: 30 sc.

Rnd 6: (2 Sc in next sc, sc in next 4 sc) around: 36 sc.

Rnds 7-11: Sc in each sc around.

Rnd 12: (Sc2tog, sc in next 4 sc) around: 30 sc.

Rnd 13: (Sc2tog, sc in next 3 sc) around: 24 sc.

Rnd 14: (Sc2tog, sc in next 2 sc) around: 18 sc.

Rnd 15: (Sc2tog, sc in next sc) around; stuff Head lightly with polyester fiberfill: 12 sc.

Rnd 16: Sc2tog around; finish off leaving a long end for sewing: 6 sc.

Thread yarn needle with long end and weave through sts on Rnd 16 *(Fig. 15, page 142)*; pull tightly to close hole and secure end, leaving the end long to sew to Blanket later.

EYE PATCH

Rnd 1 (Right side): With Brown, using smaller size hook and an adjustable loop, ch 1, 6 sc in ring, pull tail to close ring; place marker to mark beginning of the rnd.

Note: Mark Rnd 1 as right side.

Rnd 2: 2 Sc in each sc around; slip st in next sc and finish off leaving a long end for sewing.

EAR (Make 2)

With smaller size hook, using Brown and leaving a long end for sewing, ch 4.

Row 1 (Wrong side): Sc in second ch from hook and in last 2 chs: 3 sc.

Note: Mark the back of any stitch on Row 1 to mark **right** side.

Rows 2-4: Ch 1, turn; sc in each sc across.

Row 5: Ch 1, turn; sc in first sc, 2 sc in next sc, sc in last sc: 4 sc.

Rows 6-9: Ch 1, turn; sc in each sc across.

Row 10: Turn; slip st in each sc across; finish off.

ARM (Make 2)

Rnd 1 (Right side): With Tan, using smaller size hook and an adjustable loop, ch 1, 6 sc in ring, pull tail to close ring; place marker to mark beginning of the rnd.

Note: Mark Rnd 1 as **right** side.

Rnd 2: 2 Sc in each sc around: 12 sc.

Rnds 3 and 4: Sc in each sc around.

Rnd 5: (Sc2tog, sc in next 2 sc) 3 times: 9 sc.

Rnds 6-9: Sc in each sc around; at end of Rnd 9, slip st in next sc and finish off leaving a long end for sewing.

Stuff Arm lightly with polyester fiberfill.

FINISHING

Using photo as a guide:
With backstitch and Black *(Fig. 17, page 143)*, add U-shaped eye to Eye Patch; with long end from Eye Patch, sew to Head. Backstitch second eye on Head.
With straight stitch and Black *(Fig. 18, page 143)*, add upside-down triangle for nose; then fill triangle with satin stitch *(Fig. 19a, page 143)*.
With Black, backstitch remaining facial features.
Sew Ears to Head with long Brown ends.
Sew Arms along Rnd 15 on each side of Head.
With long end from Head, sew to center of Blanket.

Design by Yolanda Soto-Lopez.

KITTY LOVIE

 EASY

Finished Size: Blanket - 13½" (34.5 cm)

GAUGE INFORMATION
In Blanket pattern,
(3 dc, ch 2) 3 times = 4" (10 cm);
4 rnds = 2¾" (7 cm)
Gauge Swatch: 3¼" (8.25 cm) square
Work Blanket through Rnd 2: 24 dc and 8 sps.

STITCH GUIDE
SINGLE CROCHET 2 TOGETHER
(abbreviated sc2tog)
Pull up a loop in each of next 2 sts, YO and draw through all 3 loops on hook **(counts as one sc)**.

BLANKET
Note: Use larger size hook for entire Blanket.

With larger size hook and Light Brown, ch 4; join with slip st to form a ring.

Rnd 1 (Right side): Ch 3 **(counts as first dc, now and throughout)**, 2 dc in ring, ch 3, (3 dc in ring, ch 3) 3 times; join with slip st to first dc: 12 dc and 4 ch-3 sps.

Note: Loop a short piece of yarn around any stitch to mark Rnd 1 as **right** side.

Rnd 2: Slip st in next 2 dc and in next ch-3 sp, ch 3, (2 dc, ch 3, 3 dc) in same sp **(corner made)**, ch 2, ★ (3 dc, ch 3, 3 dc) in next ch-3 sp **(corner made)**, ch 2; repeat from ★ 2 times **more**; join with slip st to first dc, finish off: 24 dc and 8 sps.

Rnd 3: With **right** side facing, join White with dc in any corner ch-3 sp *(see Joining With Dc, page 139)*; (2 dc, ch 3, 3 dc) in same corner sp, ch 2, 3 dc in next ch-2 sp, ch 2, ★ (3 dc, ch 3, 3 dc) in next corner ch-3 sp, ch 2, 3 dc in next ch-2 sp, ch 2; repeat from ★ 2 times **more**; join with slip st to first dc: 36 dc and 12 sps.

SHOPPING LIST

Yarn
(Medium Weight) [4]
[3.5 ounces, 170 yards (100 grams, 156 meters) per skein]:
☐ Light Brown - 1 skein
☐ White - 1 skein
☐ Black - small amount

Crochet Hooks
☐ Size F (3.75 mm) (for Head, Ears, Muzzle & Arms) **and**
☐ Size J (6 mm) (for Blanket) **or** sizes needed for gauge

Additional Supplies
☐ Polyester fiberfill
☐ Yarn needle

Rnd 4: Slip st in next 2 dc and in next corner ch-3 sp, ch 3, (2 dc, ch 3, 3 dc) in same corner sp, ch 2, ★ (3 dc in next ch-2 sp, ch 2) across to next corner ch-3 sp, (3 dc, ch 3, 3 dc) in corner sp, ch 2; repeat from ★ 2 times **more**, (3 dc in next ch-2 sp, ch 2) across; join with slip st to first dc, finish off: 48 dc and 16 sps.

Rnd 5: With **right** side facing, join Light Brown with dc in any corner ch-3 sp; (2 dc, ch 3, 3 dc) in same corner sp, ch 2, ★ (3 dc in next ch-2 sp, ch 2) across to next corner ch-3 sp, (3 dc, ch 3, 3 dc) in corner sp, ch 2; repeat from ★ 2 times **more**, (3 dc in next ch-2 sp, ch 2) across; join with slip st to first dc: 60 dc and 20 sps.

Rnd 6: Repeat Rnd 4: 72 dc and 24 sps.

Rnd 7: With **right** side facing, join White with dc in any corner ch-3 sp; (2 dc, ch 3, 3 dc) in same corner sp, ch 2, ★ (3 dc in next ch-2 sp, ch 2) across to next corner ch-3 sp, (3 dc, ch 3, 3 dc) in corner sp, ch 2; repeat from ★ 2 times **more**, (3 dc in next ch-2 sp, ch 2) across; join with slip st to first dc: 84 dc and 28 sps.

Rnds 8-10: Repeat Rnd 4-6: 120 dc and 40 sps.

HEAD

Rnd 1 (Right side): With Light Brown, using smaller size hook and an adjustable loop *(Figs. 3a-d, page 139)*, ch 1, 6 sc in ring, pull tail to close ring; place marker to mark beginning of the rnd *(see Markers, page 140)*.

Note: Mark Rnd 1 as **right** side.

Rnd 2: 2 Sc in each sc around: 12 sc.

Rnd 3: (2 sc in next sc, sc in next sc) around: 18 sc.

Rnd 4: (2 sc in next sc, sc in next 2 sc) around: 24 sc.

Rnd 5: (2 Sc in next sc, sc in next 3 sc) around: 30 sc.

Rnd 6: (2 Sc in next sc, sc in next 4 sc) around: 36 sc.

Rnds 7-11: Sc in each sc around.

Rnd 12: (Sc2tog, sc in next 4 sc) around: 30 sc.

Rnd 13: (Sc2tog, sc in next 3 sc) around: 24 sc.

Rnd 14: (Sc2tog, sc in next 2 sc) around: 18 sc.

Rnd 15: (Sc2tog, sc in next sc) around; stuff Head lightly with polyester fiberfill: 12 sc.

Rnd 16: Sc2tog around; finish off leaving a long end for sewing: 6 sc.

Thread yarn needle with long end and weave through sts on Rnd 16 *(Fig. 15, page 142)*; pull tightly to close hole and secure end, leaving the end long to sew to Blanket later.

EAR (Make 2)
Back
Row 1 (Right side): With smaller size hook and Light Brown, ch 2; 3 hdc in second ch from hook.

Note: Mark Row 1 as **right** side.

Row 2: Ch 2, turn; hdc in first hdc, 2 hdc in next hdc, hdc in last hdc: 4 hdc.

Row 3: Ch 2, turn; hdc in first hdc, 2 hdc in each of next 2 hdc, hdc in last hdc; finish off leaving a long end for sewing.

Front
Row 1: With smaller size hook and White, ch 2; 3 sc in second ch from hook.

Row 2 (Right side): Ch 1, turn; sc in first sc, 2 sc in next sc, sc in last sc: 4 sc.

Note: Mark Row 2 as **right** side.

Row 3: Ch 1, turn; sc in each sc across.

Row 4: Ch 1, turn; sc in first sc, 2 sc in each of next 2 sc, sc in last sc; finish off leaving a long end for sewing.

Thread yarn needle with long White end. With wrong sides together, and matching sts on last row of each piece, sew Front and Back together (Light Brown end will be used later to sew Ear to Head).

MUZZLE

First Piece (Right side): With White, using smaller size hook and an adjustable loop, ch 1, 6 sc in ring, pull tail to close ring; join with slip st to first sc, finish off.

Note: Mark First Piece as **right** side.

Second Piece (Right side): Work same as First Piece leaving a long end for sewing.

Note: Mark Second Piece as **right** side.

With **right** sides facing, slightly overlap pieces and sew together to form center of Muzzle, leaving the end long to sew Muzzle to Head later.

ARM (Make 2)

Rnd 1 (Right side): With Light Brown, using smaller size hook and an adjustable loop, ch 1, 6 sc in ring, pull tail to close ring; place marker to mark beginning of the rnd.

Note: Mark Rnd 1 as **right** side.

Rnd 2: 2 sc in each sc around: 12 sc.

Rnds 3 and 4: Sc in each sc around.

Rnd 5: (Sc2tog, sc in next 2 sc) 3 times: 9 sc.

Rnds 6-9: Sc in each sc around; at end of Rnd 9, slip st in next sc and finish off leaving a long end for sewing.

Stuff Arm lightly with polyester fiberfill.

FINISHING

Using photo as a guide:
With outline stitch and Black *(Figs. 20a & b, page 143)*, add U-shaped eyes to Head.
With long end from Muzzle, sew to Head centered between Rnds 11 & 12.
With straight stitch and Black *(Fig. 18, page 143)*, add upside-down triangle for nose; then fill triangle with satin stitch *(Fig. 19a, page 143)*.
With Black, straight stitch remaining facial features.
Sew Ears to Head with long Light Brown ends. Sew Arms along Rnd 15 on each side of Head.
With long end from Head, sew to center of Blanket.

Design by Yolanda Soto-Lopez.

LACY CUFF BOOTS

 EASY

SIZE INFORMATION
Small: 2" wide x 3" long
  (5 cm x 7.5 cm)
Medium: 2" wide x 3½" long
  (5 cm x 9 cm)

Size Note: We have printed the instructions for the sizes in different colors to make it easier for you to find:
• Size Small in Blue
• Size Medium in Pink
Instructions in Black apply to both sizes.

GAUGE INFORMATION
Gauge Swatch: 2" wide x 3{3½}" long
  [5 cm x 7.5{9} cm]
Work same as Sole.

STITCH GUIDE
TREBLE CROCHET *(abbreviated tr)*
YO twice, insert hook in st indicated, YO and pull up a loop (4 loops on hook), (YO and draw through 2 loops on hook) 3 times.

SINGLE CROCHET 2 TOGETHER
  (abbreviated sc2tog)
Pull up a loop in each of next 2 sts, YO and draw through all 3 loops on hook **(counts as one sc)**.

DOUBLE CROCHET 2 TOGETHER
  (abbreviated dc2tog)
  (uses next 2 sts)
★ YO, insert hook in **next** st, YO and pull up a loop, YO and draw through 2 loops on hook; repeat from ★ once **more**, YO and draw through all 3 loops on hook **(counts as one dc)**.

BOOT (Make 2)
Sole (Make 2 for each boot)
With Grey, ch 8{10}.

Rnd 1 (Right side): Sc in second ch from hook and in each ch across to last ch, 4 hdc in last ch; working in free loops of beginning ch *(Fig. 6b, page 140)*, sc in next 5{7} chs, 3 sc in next ch; join with slip st to first sc: 18{22} sts.

Note: Loop a short piece of yarn around any stitch to mark Rnd 1 as **right** side.

Rnd 2: Ch 1, sc in same st as joining and in next 3{5} sc, hdc in next 2 sc, 2 dc in each of next 4 hdc, hdc in next 2 sc, sc in next 3{5} sc, 2 sc in each of last 3 sc; join with slip st to first sc: 25{29} sts.

SHOPPING LIST

Yarn
(Medium Weight)
☐ Grey - 80 yards (73 meters)
☐ Lavender - 30 yards
(27.5 meters)
☐ White - small amount
☐ Pink - small amount

Crochet Hook
☐ Size F (3.75 mm)
  or size needed for gauge

Additional Supplies
☐ Split ring marker
  or scrap yarn
☐ Yarn needle

Rnd 3: Ch 2 **(does not count as a st)**, hdc in same st as joining and in next 6{8} sts, 2 hdc in next dc, (hdc in next dc, 2 hdc in next dc) 3 times, hdc in next 5{7} sts, (sc in next sc, 2 sc in next sc) 3 times; join with slip st to first hdc, finish off: 32{36} sts.

On one Sole for each boot, place split ring marker or scrap yarn in Front Loop Only of first hdc made on Rnd 3 for st placement *(Fig. 5, page 140)*.

Joining: Hold two Soles with **wrong** sides together, matching sts, and marked Sole on bottom. Do **not** begin with slip knot on hook. Holding Lavender to the back and working through **both** loops of **both** pieces, insert hook in any st on Rnd 3, YO and pull up a loop, slip st in each st around; cut yarn. Remove hook from loop. Insert hook from **back** to **front** through center of first st, hook loop and draw through, YO and pull end through loop.

SIDES & TOE

Rnd 1 (Right side)**:** With marked Sole away from you and working in Back Loops Only, join Grey with sc in marked loop *(see Joining With Sc, page 138)*; remove marker, sc in each st around; drop Grey, with Lavender, join with slip st to first sc *(Fig. 7a, page 140)*: 32{36} sc.

Rnd 2: Ch 1, sc in both loops of each sc around; drop Lavender, with Grey, join with slip st to first sc.

Rnd 3: Ch 1, sc in same st as joining and in next 11{13} sc, dc2tog 8 times, sc in next 4{6} sc; drop Grey, with Lavender, join with slip st to first sc: 24{28} sts.

Rnd 4: Ch 1, sc in same st as joining and in next 11{13} sc, dc2tog 4 times, sc in next 4{6} sc; drop Lavender, with Grey, join with slip st to first sc: 20{24} sts.

Rnd 5: Ch 1, sc in same st as joining and in next 11{13} sc, dc2tog twice, sc in last 4{6} sc; drop Grey, with Lavender, join with slip st to first sc: 18{22} sc.

Rnd 6: Ch 1, sc in same st as joining and in next 11{13} sc, sc2tog, sc in last 4{6} sc; cut Lavender, with Grey, join with slip st to first sc: 17{21} sc.

Rnd 7: Ch 1, sc in each sc around; do not join, place marker to indicate beginning of rnd *(see Markers, page 140)*.

Rnds 8-13: Sc in each sc around.

Slip st in next sc, finish off.

Lacy Cuff

Size Small Only - Rnd 1: With **wrong** side facing and working in Back Loops Only, join Lavender with sc in same st as slip st; (sc in next 3 sc, 2 sc in next sc) around; join with slip st to first sc: 21 sc.

Size Medium Only - Rnd 1: With **wrong** side facing and working in Back Loops Only, join Lavender with sc in same st as slip st; sc in next 5 sc, 2 sc in next sc, (sc in next 6 sc, 2 sc in next sc) twice; join with slip st to first sc: 24 sc.

Both Sizes - Rnd 2: Ch 4 **(counts as first tr)**, turn; skip next 4 sc, tr in next sc, ch 1, working in **front** of tr just made *(Fig. 9, page 141)*, tr in third skipped sc, ★ skip next 2 sc, tr in next sc, ch 1, working in front of tr just made, tr in first skipped sc; repeat from ★ around, working **behind** first tr *(Fig. 9, page 141)*, tr in second skipped sc, ch 1; join with slip st to first tr: 14{16} tr and 7{8} ch-1 sps.

Rnd 3: Ch 1, turn; sc in same st as joining and in each ch-1 sp and each tr around; join with slip st to first sc: 21{24} sc.

Rnd 4: Repeat Rnd 2.

Rnd 5: Ch 3, turn; slip st in same st as joining, (slip st, ch 3, slip st) in each ch-1 sp and in each tr around; finish off.

Fold Cuff down.

Flower

With Pink, ch 4; join with slip st to form a ring.

Rnd 1 (Right side)**:** 6 Sc in ring; join with slip st to first sc, finish off leaving a long end for sewing.

Note: Mark Rnd 1 as **right** side.

Rnd 2: With **right** side facing, join White with slip st in first sc, ch 2, (dc, ch 1, slip st) in same st, (slip st, ch 2, dc, ch 1, slip st) in each sc around; join with slip st to joining slip st, finish off.

Using photo as a guide for placement, sew a Flower to each Cuff having a right and left boot.

Design by Kristi Simpson.

KALEIDOSCOPE THROW

 EASY

Finished Size: 46½" (118 cm) square

GAUGE INFORMATION
Gauge Swatch: 4½" (11.5 cm) square
Work same as Square.

STITCH GUIDE
FRONT POST DOUBLE CROCHET
(abbreviated FPdc)
YO, insert hook from **front** to **back** around post of st indicated *(Fig. 10, page 141)*, YO and pull up a loop (3 loops on hook), (YO and draw through 2 loops on hook) twice.

BACK POST DOUBLE CROCHET
(abbreviated BPdc)
YO, insert hook from **back** to **front** around post of st indicated *(Fig. 10, page 141)*, YO and pull up a loop (3 loops on hook), (YO and draw through 2 loops on hook) twice.

DOUBLE CROCHET 2 TOGETHER
(abbreviated dc2tog) (uses next 2 dc)
★ YO, insert hook in **next** dc, YO and pull up a loop, YO and draw through 2 loops on hook; repeat from ★ once **more**, YO and draw through all 3 loops on hook (**counts as one dc**).

DOUBLE CROCHET 3 TOGETHER
(abbreviated dc3tog) (uses next 3 dc)
★ YO, insert hook in **next** dc, YO and pull up a loop, YO and draw through 2 loops on hook; repeat from ★ 2 times **more**, YO and draw through all 4 loops on hook (**counts as one dc**).

SQUARE (Make 100 total)
Make 32 each of Square A and Square C, and 36 of Square B.

Rows	A	B	C
1-4	Blue	Dk Blue	Lt Blue
5-8	Yellow	Yellow	Yellow
9-12	Lt Blue	Blue	Dk Blue

Row 1: With first color indicated, ch 4, 3 dc in fourth ch from hook (**3 skipped chs count as first dc**): 4 dc.

SHOPPING LIST

Yarn
(Medium Weight) [4]
[7 ounces, 426 yards (197 grams, 389 meters) per skein]:
☐ Yellow - 3 skeins
☐ Blue - 2 skeins
☐ Light Blue - 1 skein
☐ Dark Blue - 1 skein

Crochet Hook
☐ Size H (5 mm)
   or size needed for gauge

Additional Supplies
☐ Yarn needle

KALEIDOSCOPE THROW

Row 2 (Right side): Ch 3 **(counts as first dc, now and throughout)**, turn; dc in first dc, work FPdc around each of next 2 dc, 2 dc in last dc: 6 sts.

Note: Loop a short piece of yarn around any stitch to mark Row 2 as **right** side.

Row 3: Ch 3, turn; 2 dc in first dc, dc in next dc, work BPdc around next FPdc, ch 1, work BPdc around next FPdc, dc in next dc, 3 dc in last dc: 10 sts and one ch-1 sp.

Row 4: Ch 3, turn; 2 dc in first dc, dc in next 3 dc, work FPdc around next BPdc, ch 1, work FPdc around next BPdc, dc in next 3 dc, 3 dc in last dc changing to next color in last dc *(Fig. 7d, page 140)*: 14 sts and one ch-1 sp.

Row 5: Ch 3, turn; 2 dc in first dc, dc in next 5 dc, work BPdc around next FPdc, ch 1, work BPdc around next FPdc, dc in next 5 dc, 3 dc in last dc: 18 sts and one ch-1 sp.

Row 6: Ch 3, turn; 2 dc in first dc, dc in next 7 dc, work FPdc around next BPdc, ch 1, work FPdc around next BPdc, dc in next 7 dc, 3 dc in last dc: 22 sts and one ch-1 sp.

Row 7: Ch 2, turn; dc2tog, dc in next 7 dc, work BPdc around next FPdc, ch 1, work BPdc around next FPdc, dc in next 7 dc, dc3tog: 18 sts and one ch-1 sp.

Row 8: Ch 2, turn; dc2tog, dc in next 5 dc, work FPdc around next BPdc, ch 1, work FPdc around next BPdc, dc in next 5 dc, dc3tog changing to next color: 14 sts and one ch-1 sp.

Row 9: Ch 2, turn; dc2tog, dc in next 3 dc, work BPdc around next FPdc, ch 1, work BPdc around next FPdc, dc in next 3 dc, dc3tog: 10 sts and one ch-1 sp.

Row 10: Ch 2, turn; dc2tog, dc in next dc, work FPdc around next BPdc, ch 1, work FPdc around next BPdc, dc in next dc, dc3tog: 6 sts and one ch-1 sp.

Row 11: Ch 2, turn; dc in next dc, work BPdc around each of next 2 FPdc, dc2tog: 4 sts.

Row 12: Ch 2, turn; ★ YO, insert hook from front to back around post of next BPdc, YO and pull up a loop, YO and draw through 2 loops on hook; repeat from ★ once **more**, YO, insert hook in last dc, YO and pull up a loop (5 loops on hook), YO and draw through 2 loops on hook, YO and draw through all 4 loops on hook; finish off.

ASSEMBLY

Using Placement Diagram as a guide, with **wrong** sides together, whipstitch Squares *(Fig. 13c, page 142)* together forming 10 vertical strips of 10 Squares each, beginning in first corner and ending in next corner; then join strips together in same manner.

EDGING

Rnd 1: With **right** side facing, join Blue with sc in any corner *(see Joining With Sc, page 138)*; 2 sc in same st, ★ † work 12 sc evenly spaced across same Square, work 13 sc evenly spaced across each of next 9 Squares †, 3 sc in corner; repeat from ★ 2 times **more**, then repeat from † to † once; join with slip st to first sc: 528 sc.

Rnd 2: Ch 3, (sc, dc, sc) in next sc, ★ dc in next sc, (sc in next sc, dc in next sc) across to next corner sc, (sc, dc, sc) in corner sc; repeat from ★ 2 times **more**, (dc in next sc, sc in next sc) across; join with slip st to first dc: 536 sts.

Rnd 3: Ch 1, sc in same st as joining, dc in next sc, (sc, dc, sc) in next dc, ★ dc in next sc, (sc in next dc, dc in next sc) across to next corner dc, (sc, dc, sc) in corner dc; repeat from ★ 2 times **more**, dc in next sc, (sc in next sc, dc in next sc) across; join with slip st to first sc, finish off.

Design by Jennine DeMoss.

HIGH-TOP SNEAKERS

 EASY

SIZE INFORMATION
Small: 2" wide x 3" long
  (5 cm x 7.5 cm)
Medium: 2" wide x 3½" long
  (5 cm x 9 cm)

Size Note: We have printed the instructions for the sizes in different colors to make it easier for you to find:
• Size Small in Blue
• Size Medium in Pink
Instructions in Black apply to both sizes.

GAUGE INFORMATION
Gauge Swatch: 2" wide x 3{3½}" long
  [5 cm x 7.5{9} cm]
Work same as Sole.

STITCH GUIDE
SINGLE CROCHET 2 TOGETHER
  (abbreviated sc2tog)
Pull up a loop in each of next 2 sts, YO and draw through all 3 loops on hook **(counts as one sc)**.

DOUBLE CROCHET 2 TOGETHER
  (*abbreviated dc2tog*) (uses next 2 sts)
★ YO, insert hook in next st, YO and pull up a loop, YO and draw through 2 loops on hook; repeat from ★ once **more**, YO and draw through all 3 loops on hook **(counts as one dc)**.

SNEAKER (Make 2)
Sole (Make 2 for each sneaker)
With White, ch 8{10}.

Rnd 1 (Right side): Sc in second ch from hook and in each ch across to last ch, 4 hdc in last ch; working in free loops of beginning ch (*Fig. 6b, page 140*), sc in next 5{7} chs, 3 sc in next ch; join with slip st to first sc: 18{22} sts.

Note: Loop a short piece of yarn around any stitch to mark Rnd 1 as right side.

SHOPPING LIST

Yarn
(Medium Weight)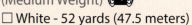
☐ White - 52 yards (47.5 meters)
☐ Blue - 52 yards (47.5 meters)
☐ Red - small amount

Crochet Hook
☐ Size F (3.75 mm)
  or size needed for gauge

Additional Supplies
☐ Split ring marker
  or scrap yarn
☐ Yarn needle

Rnd 2: Ch 1, sc in same st as joining and in next 3{5} sc, hdc in next 2 sc, 2 dc in each of next 4 hdc, hdc in next 2 sc, sc in next 3{5} sc, 2 sc in each of last 3 sc; join with slip st to first sc: 25{29} sts.

Rnd 3: Ch 2 (**does not count as a st, now and throughout**), hdc in same st as joining and in next 6{8} sts, 2 hdc in next dc, (hdc in next dc, 2 hdc in next dc) 3 times, hdc in next 5{7} sts, (sc in next sc, 2 sc in next sc) 3 times; join with slip st to first hdc, finish off: 32{36} sts.

On one Sole, place split ring marker or scrap yarn in Front Loop Only of fifth{seventh} hdc made on Rnd 3 for st placement (**Fig. 5, page 140**).

Joining: Hold two Soles with **wrong** sides together, matching sts, and marked Sole on bottom. Do **not** begin with slip knot on hook. Holding Red to the back and working through **both** loops of **both** pieces, insert hook in any st on Rnd 3, YO and pull up a loop, slip st in each st around; cut yarn. Remove hook from loop. Insert hook from **back** to **front** through center of first st, hook loop and draw through, YO and pull end through loop.

Sides
Row 1 (Right side): With marked Sole away from you and working in Back Loops Only, join Blue with sc in marked loop (*see Joining With Sc, page 138*); remove marker, sc in next 15{19} sts, leave remaining 16 sts unworked: 16{20} sc.

Row 2: Ch 2, turn; dc in both loops of each sc across.

Row 3: Ch 1, turn; sc in each dc across.

Rows 4 thru 6{8}: Repeat Rows 2 and 3, 1{2} time(s); then repeat Row 2 once **more**.

Finish off.

Trim: With **right** side facing, join Red with slip st in first dc on Sides; slip st in each dc across; finish off.

Toe
Row 1: With **right** side facing and working in Back Loops Only of Sole, join White with sc in first unworked st; sc in each sc across: 16 sc.

Row 2: Ch 1, turn; working in both loops, sc in first sc, hdc in next 3 sc, dc in next 8 sc, hdc in next 3 sc, sc in last sc.

Row 3: Turn; working in Back Loops Only and beginning in first sc, sc2tog twice, dc2tog 4 times, sc2tog twice: 8 sts.

Row 4: Ch 1, turn; working in both loops, sc in first 2 sc, dc in next 4 dc, sc in last 2 sc; finish off.

Tongue
Row 1: With **right** side facing, join Blue with sc in first sc on Toe; sc in each st across.

Rows 2 thru 9{11}: Ch 1, turn; sc in each sc across.

Finish off.

With White, sew end of first 3 rows on Sides to end of rows on Toe.

Laces
With White, ch 80{85}; finish off.

Using photo as a guide for placement and beginning at the bottom of the Sides, weave Laces through end of rows.

Design by Kristi Simpson.

DOUBLE DIP BLANKET

 **EASY**

Shown on page 3.

Finished Size: 37½" x 44½" (95.5 cm x 113 cm)

GAUGE INFORMATION
5 Blocks (side by side) = 3¼"
 (8.25 cm)
Gauge Swatch: 3¼" x 3¼" x 4½"
 (8.25 cm x 8.25 cm x 11.5 cm)
Work same as Body for 5 rows:
5 Blocks.

STITCH GUIDE
BEGINNING BLOCK
Ch 6, turn; dc in fourth ch from hook and in next 2 chs.
BLOCK
Slip st in ch-3 sp of previous Block *Fig. A)*, ch 3, 3 dc in same sp *(Fig. B)*.

Fig. A   Fig. B

BODY
Body is worked diagonally.

Row 1 (Right side): With White, ch 6, dc in fourth ch from hook and in last 2 chs: one Block.

Note: Loop a short piece of yarn around any stitch to mark Row 1 as **right** side **and** bottom corner.

Row 2: Work Beginning Block, slip st in ch-3 sp on first Block, ch 3, 3 dc in same sp: 2 Blocks.

Row 3: Work Beginning Block, slip st in ch-3 sp on first Block, ch 3, 3 dc in same sp, work Block: 3 Blocks.

Rows 4-32: Work Beginning Block, slip st in ch-3 sp on first Block, ch 3, 3 dc in same sp, work Blocks across: 32 Blocks.

Row 33: Work Beginning Block, slip st in ch-3 sp on first Block, ch 3, 3 dc in same sp, work 27 Blocks, changing to Tan in last dc made (*Fig. 7d, page 140*), work Block changing to White in last dc made, work Blocks across: 33 Blocks.

Always change colors in same manner, using bobbins for small sections of color. Keep unused color to **wrong** side of work; do **not** cut yarn until color is no longer needed.

Continue to follow Chart throughout.

SHOPPING LIST

Yarn
(Light Weight) [3]
[5 ounces, 362 yards
(140 grams, 331 meters)
per skein]:
☐ White - 5 skeins
☐ Pink - 1 skein
[4.2 ounces, 310 yards
(120 grams, 283 meters)
per skein]:
☐ Variegated - 1 skein
[1.75 ounces, 161 yards
(50 grams, 147 meters)
per skein]:
☐ Tan - 1 skein

Crochet Hook
☐ Size G (4 mm)
 or size needed for gauge

Additional Supplies
☐ Bobbins

CHART

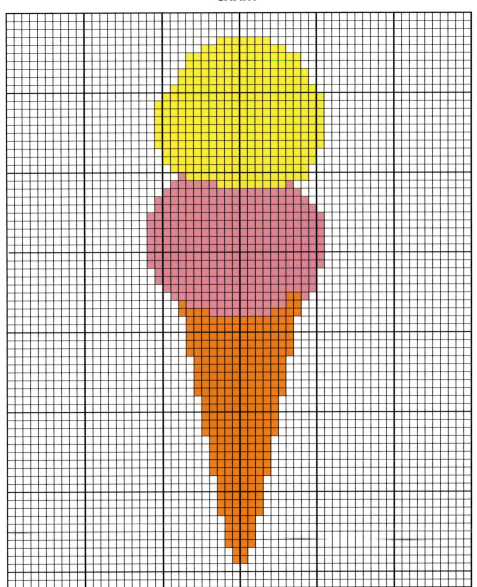

Rows 34-60: Work Beginning Block, slip st in ch-3 sp on first Block, ch 3, 3 dc in same sp, work Blocks across: 60 Blocks.

Row 61: Work Beginning Block, slip st in ch-3 sp on first Block, ch 3, 3 dc in same sp, work Blocks across to last Block, slip st in ch-3 sp on last Block.

Row 62: Turn; slip st in first 3 dc and in next ch-3 sp, ch 3, 3 dc in same sp, work Blocks across.

Rows 63-72: Repeat Rows 61 and 62, 5 times.

Rows 73-128: Turn; slip st in first 3 dc and in next ch-3 sp, ch 3, 3 dc in same sp, work Blocks across to last Block, slip st in ch-3 sp on last Block: 4 Blocks.

Row 129: Turn; slip st in first 3 dc and in next ch-3 sp, ch 3, 3 dc in same sp, work 2 Blocks, slip st in ch-3 sp on last Block: 3 Blocks.

Row 130: Turn; slip st in first 3 dc and in next ch-3 sp, ch 3, 3 dc in same sp, work Block, slip st in ch-3 sp on last Block: 2 Blocks.

Row 131: Turn; slip st in first 3 dc and in next ch-3 sp, ch 3, 3 dc in same sp, slip st in ch-3 sp on last Block; do **not** finish off: one Block.

EDGING

Rnd 1: Ch 1, do **not** turn; sc evenly around entire Body working 3 sc in each corner; join with slip st to first sc.

Rnd 2: Ch 1, sc in each sc around working 3 sc in center sc of each corner 3-sc group; join with slip st to first sc, finish off.

Rnd 3: With **right** side facing, join Pink with sc in center sc of any corner 3-sc group *(see Joining With Sc, page 138)*; 2 sc in same st as joining, sc in each sc around working 3 sc in center sc of each corner 3-sc group; join with slip st to first sc.

Rnd 4: Ch 1, working from **left** to **right**, work reverse sc in each sc around *(Figs. 12a-d, page 141)*; join with slip st to first st, finish off.

Design by Becky Stevens.

GIRAFFE BIB

EASY

Finished Size: 7½" wide x 6¾" long (19 cm x 17 cm) excluding Ears & Horns

GAUGE INFORMATION
11 sc and 12.5 rows = 3" (7.5 cm)
Gauge Swatch: 3" wide x 2⅞" high (7.5 cm x 7.25 cm)
With Yellow, ch 12.
Row 1: Sc in second ch from hook and in each ch across: 11 sc.
Rows 2-12: Ch 1, turn; sc in each sc across.
Finish off.

STITCH GUIDE
SINGLE CROCHET 2 TOGETHER
   (abbreviated sc2tog)
Pull up a loop in each of next 2 sc, YO and draw through all 3 loops on hook **(counts as one sc)**.

HEAD
With Yellow and beginning at top of Head, ch 13; place marker in second ch from hook for Trim placement.

Row 1 (Right side): 2 Sc in second ch from hook, sc in each ch across to last ch, 2 sc in last ch: 14 sc.

Note: Loop a short piece of yarn around any stitch to mark Row 1 as **right** side.

Rows 2-7: Ch 1, turn; 2 sc in first sc, sc in each sc across to last sc, 2 sc in last sc: 26 sc.

Rows 8-23: Ch 1, turn; sc in each sc across.

Rows 24-26: Ch 1, turn; beginning in first sc, sc2tog, sc in each sc across to last 2 sc, sc2tog: 20 sc.

Edging: Ch 1, turn; beginning in first sc, sc2tog, sc in each sc across to last 2 sc, sc2tog; sc evenly across end of rows; working in free loops of beginning ch *(Fig. 6b, page 140)*, sc in first ch, place marker in sc just made for Tie placement, sc in each ch across to marked ch, remove marker and place marker in last sc made for Tie placement, sc in next ch; sc evenly across end of rows; join with slip st to first sc, finish off.

SHOPPING LIST

Yarn
(Medium Weight)
[1.75 ounces, 80 yards (50 grams, 73 meters) per ball]:
☐ Yellow - 60 yards (55 meters)
☐ Tan - 35 yards (32 meters)
☐ Brown - small amount

Crochet Hook
☐ Size G (4 mm)
   or size needed for gauge

Additional Supplies
☐ Yarn needle

GIRAFFE BIB

Tie

With **right** side facing, join Yellow with slip st in either marked sc on Edging, remove marker; ch 52, hdc in back ridge of second ch from hook *(Fig. 4, page 140)* and each ch across; slip st in next sc on Edging, finish off.

Repeat for second Tie in remaining marked sc.

FEATURES

Ear (Make 2)

With Yellow and beginning at tip, ch 2.

Row 1 (Right side): 2 Sc in second ch from hook.

Note: Mark Row 1 as **right** side.

Row 2: Ch 1, turn; 2 sc in each sc across: 4 sc.

Row 3: Ch 1, turn; 2 sc in first sc, sc in next 2 sc, 2 sc in last sc: 6 sc.

Rows 4-6: Ch 1, turn; sc in each sc across.

Row 7: Ch 1, turn; beginning in first sc, sc2tog, sc in next 2 sc, sc2tog; finish off leaving a long end for sewing.

Muzzle

With Tan, ch 19.

Row 1 (Wrong side): Working in back ridges of beginning ch, 2 sc in second ch from hook, sc in each ch across to last ch, 2 sc in last ch: 20 sc.

Note: Mark the back of Row 1 as **right** side.

Rows 2 and 3: Ch 1, turn; 2 sc in first sc, sc in each sc across to last sc, 2 sc in last sc: 24 sc.

Rows 4-8: Ch 1, turn; sc in each sc across.

Rows 9-12: Ch 1, turn; beginning in first sc, sc2tog, sc in each sc across to last 2 sc, sc2tog: 16 sc.

Finish off leaving a long end for sewing.

With a double strand of Brown, embroider a line around the edge of the Muzzle using running stitch *(Fig. 21, page 143)*.

Horn (Make 2)

With Tan, ch 2.

Rnd 1 (Right side): 6 Sc in second ch from hook; join with slip st to first sc.

Note: Mark Rnd 1 as **right** side.

Rnd 2: Ch 1, 2 sc in same st as joining and in each sc around; join with slip st to first sc: 12 sc.

Begin working in rows.

Row 1: Ch 1, turn; sc in first 2 sc, leave remaining 10 sc unworked.

Rows 2 and 3: Ch 1, turn; sc in first 2 sc.

Finish off leaving a long end for sewing.

Eye (Make 2)

With Brown, ch 2.

Rnd 1 (Right side): 6 Sc in second ch from hook; join with slip st to first sc, finish off leaving a long end for sewing.

FINISHING

Using photo as a guide for placement and with **right** side of all pieces facing:
Sew Ears to Head Edging.
With a double strand of Brown, backstitch mouth on Muzzle. With a double strand of Brown, straight stitch an "X" for each nostril.
Sew Muzzle, Horns and Eyes to Head.

Design by Kristi Simpson.

HAT & MOCCASINS

 EASY

GAUGE INFORMATION
Hat
Gauge Swatch: 3" (7.5 cm) square
With larger size hook and Grey, ch 11.
Row 1: Sc in second ch from hook and in each ch across: 10 sc.
Rows 2-12: Ch 1, turn; sc in each sc across.
Finish off.
Moccasins
Gauge Swatch: 2" wide x 3{3½}" long/5 cm x 7.5{9} cm
With smaller size hook, work same as Sole: 32{36} sts.

STITCH GUIDE
SPLIT SINGLE CROCHET
   (abbreviated Split sc)
Insert hook between legs of next st **(Fig. A)**, YO and pull up a loop, YO and draw through both loops on hook.

Fig. A

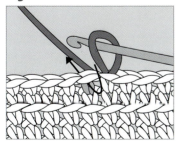

SINGLE CROCHET 2 TOGETHER
   (abbreviated sc2tog)
Pull up a loop in each of next 2 sts, YO and draw through all 3 loops on hook **(counts as one sc)**.

DOUBLE CROCHET 2 TOGETHER
   (abbreviated dc2tog) (uses next 2 sts)
★ YO, insert hook in next st, YO and pull up a loop, YO and draw through 2 loops on hook; repeat from ★ once more, YO and draw through all 3 loops on hook (counts as one dc).

HAT
Finished Size: 14" (35.5 cm) circumference

Use larger size hook throughout.

With Grey and leaving a long end for sewing, ch 46.

Rnd 1 (Right side): Sc in second ch from hook and in each ch across; join with slip st to first sc: 45 sc.

Note: Loop a short piece of yarn around any stitch to mark Rnd 1 as **right** side.

Rnd 2: Ch 1, work Split sc in each sc around; join with slip st to first Split sc.

SHOPPING LIST

Yarn
(Medium Weight) [4]
[4 ounces, 203 yards
(113 grams, 186 meters)
per skein]:
☐ Grey - 1 skein
☐ Green - 1 skein
☐ Blue - 1 skein
☐ Gold - 1 skein

Crochet Hooks
☐ Size F (3.75 mm) **and**
☐ Size H (5 mm)
   or sizes needed for gauge

Additional Supplies
☐ Split ring marker
   or scrap yarn
☐ Yarn needle

Rnds 3 and 4: Ch 1, work Split sc in each Split sc around; join with slip st to first Split sc.

Rnd 5: Ch 1, sc in Back Loop Only *(Fig. 5, page 140)* of each st around; do not join, place marker to indicate beginning of rnd *(see Markers, page 140)*.

Rnds 6-17: Sc in each sc around.

Rnd 18: (Sc2tog, sc in next 3 sc) around: 36 sc.

Rnd 19: (Sc2tog, sc in next 2 sc) around: 27 sc.

Rnd 20: (Sc2tog, sc in next sc) around: 18 sc.

Rnd 21: Sc2tog around: 9 sc.

Rnd 22: Sc in each sc around; slip st in next sc, finish off leaving a long end for sewing.

Thread yarn needle with long end and weave needle through sts on Rnd 22 *(Fig. 15, page 142)*, gather tightly and secure end.

Thread yarn needle with beginning end and sew through chs at base of first and last sc; secure end.

DUPLICATE SPLIT SC

Duplicate Split sc is worked over the first Split sc rnd (Rnd 2). Each stitch forms a V and you want to completely cover that V so that the design appears to have been worked into the fabric. Thread a yarn needle with an 18" (45.5 cm) length of Blue.

With **right** side facing and beginning at first stitch on Rnd 2, bring the needle up from the **wrong** side between the strands of yarn on Rnd 2 at the base of the V, leaving an end to be woven in later *(Fig. B)*.

Fig. B

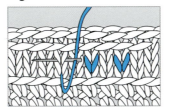

Follow the right side of the V up and insert the needle from **right** to **left** under the strands of the V immediately above, keeping the yarn on top of the stitch *(Fig. C)*, and draw through.

Fig. C

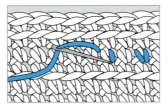

Insert the needle back through the bottom of the same stitch where the first stitch began (**duplicate Split sc completed**).
Work over every other stitch around, matching tension of fabric to avoid puckering.

With Gold, work duplicate Split sc over each unworked stitch of Rnd 2. Repeat duplicate Split sc on Rnd 3 alternating colors.

With double strand of Green, weave through sts on Rnd 1; secure ends to **wrong** side.

With double strand of Green, weave through sts on Rnd 4. Secure ends of one strand on **wrong** side; with remaining strand, tie ends in a bow.

MOCCASIN (Make 2)
SIZE INFORMATION
Small: 2" wide x 3" long
 (5 cm x 7.5 cm)
Medium: 2" wide x 3½" long
 (5 cm x 9 cm)

Size Note: We have printed the instructions for the sizes in different colors to make it easier for you to find:
• Size Small in Blue
• Size Medium in Pink
Instructions in Black apply to both sizes.

Use smaller size hook throughout.

Sole (Make one in Grey and one in Green for **each** moccasin)

Ch 8{10}.

Rnd 1 (Right side): Sc in second ch from hook and in each ch across to last ch, 4 hdc in last ch; working in free loops of beginning ch *(Fig. 6b, page 140)*, sc in next 5{7} chs, 3 sc in next ch; join with slip st to first sc: 18{22} sts.

Note: Loop a short piece of yarn around any stitch to mark Rnd 1 as **right** side.

Rnd 2: Ch 1, sc in same st as joining and in next 3{5} sc, hdc in next 2 sc, 2 dc in each of next 4 hdc, hdc in next 2 sc, sc in next 3{5} sc, 2 sc in each of last 3 sc; join with slip st to first sc: 25{29} sts.

HAT & MOCCASINS

Rnd 3: Ch 2 (**does not count as a st**), hdc in same st as joining and in next 6{8} sts, 2 hdc in next dc, (hdc in next dc, 2 hdc in next dc) 3 times, hdc in next 5{7} sts, (sc in next sc, 2 sc in next sc) 3 times; join with slip st to first hdc, finish off: 32{36} sts.

On Grey Sole, place split ring marker or scrap yarn in Front Loop Only of first hdc made on Rnd 3 for st placement *(Fig. 5, page 140)*.

Joining: Hold two Soles with **wrong** sides together, matching sts, and Green Sole facing you. Do **not** begin with slip knot on hook. Holding Grey to the back and working through **both** loops of **both** pieces, insert hook in any st on Rnd 3, YO and pull up a loop, slip st in each st around; cut yarn. Remove hook from loop. Insert hook from **back** to **front** through center of first st, hook loop and draw through, YO and pull end through loop.

Sides & Toe

Rnd 1 (Right side): With Grey Sole away from you and working in Back Loops Only, join Grey with sc in marked loop *(see Joining With Sc, page 138)*; remove marker, sc in each st around; join with slip st to first sc: 32{36} sc.

Rnd 2: Ch 1, sc in both loops of each sc around; join with slip st to first sc.

Rnd 3: Ch 1, sc in same st as joining and in next 11{13} sc, working in Back Loops Only, dc2tog 8 times, sc in both loops of last 4{6} sc; join with slip st to first sc: 24{28} sts.

Rnd 4: Ch 1, sc in same st as joining and in next 11{13} sc, dc2tog 4 times, sc in last 4{6} sc; join with slip st to first sc: 20{24} sts.

Rnd 5: Ch 1, sc in same st as joining and in next 11{13} sc, dc2tog twice, sc in last 4{6} sc; join with slip st to first sc: 18{22} sc.

Rnds 6-11: Ch 1, sc in each sc around; join with slip st to first sc.

Rnd 12: Ch 1, sc in Back Loop Only of each sc around; join with slip st to first sc.

Rnd 13: Ch 1, work Split sc in each sc around; join with slip st to first Split sc.

Rnd 14: Ch 1, work Split sc in each Split sc around; join with slip st to first Split sc.

Rnd 15: Ch 1, sc in Back Loop Only of each st around; join with slip st to first sc, finish off.

With Blue, work duplicate Split sc over every other stitch on Rnd 13, matching tension of fabric to avoid puckering.

With Gold, work duplicate Split sc over each unworked stitch on Rnd 13.

Fringe

Cut a piece of cardboard 2" (5 cm) square. Wind Grey loosely and evenly around the cardboard until the card is filled, then cut across one end; repeat as needed.

Fold one strand of yarn in half. Insert hook from top to bottom in free loop of first stitch on Rnd 11 (unused loop after working in back loops). Draw the folded end up through the stitch and pull the loose ends through the folded end *(Fig. D)*; draw the knot up tightly *(Fig. E)*. Repeat in each stitch around. Trim the ends.

Fig. D

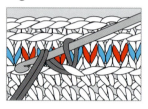

Fig. E

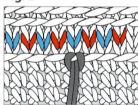

Trim

Using photo as a guide for placement and beginning at opposite sides of boots for right and left boot, weave a single strand of Green through stitches on last rnd; tie ends in a bow.

Design by Kristi Simpson.

WATER LILIES SET

 EASY

SIZE INFORMATION

BLANKET - 31½" wide x 23½" long
(80 cm x 59.5 cm)

HAT

Size: 0-6{6-12} Months

Fits Head Circumference:
13-15{16-17}"/33-38{40.5-43} cm

Size Note: We have printed the instructions for the Hat in different colors to make it easier for you to find:
• Size 0-6 Months in Blue
• Size 6-12 Months in Pink
Instructions in Black apply to both sizes.

GAUGE INFORMATION

Blanket - In pattern, one repeat
(14 sts) and 11 rows = 3" (7.5 cm)

Hat - Rnds 1 and 2 = 2" (5 cm)

Gauge Swatch: 6" wide x 3¼" high
(15.25 cm x 8.25 cm)
With Teal Ombre, ch 32.
Work same as Blanket Body for 12 rows: 29 sc.
Finish off.

BLANKET
Body

With Teal Ombre, ch 144.

Row 1 (Right side)**:** 3 Dc in fourth ch from hook **(3 skipped chs count as first dc)**, skip next 3 chs, sc in next 7 chs, ★ skip next 3 chs, 7 dc in next ch, skip next 3 chs, sc in next 7 chs; repeat from ★ across to last 4 chs, skip next 3 chs, 4 dc in last ch: 141 sts.

Note: Loop a short piece of yarn around any stitch to mark Row 1 as **right** side.

Row 2: Ch 1, turn; sc in each st across.

Row 3: Ch 1, turn; sc in first 4 sc, skip next 3 sc, 7 dc in next sc, ★ skip next 3 sc, sc in next 7 sc, skip next 3 sc, 7 dc in next sc; repeat from ★ across to last 7 sc, skip next 3 sc, sc in last 4 sc.

Row 4: Ch 1, turn; sc in each st across.

Row 5: Ch 3 **(counts as first dc, now and throughout)**, turn; 3 dc in first sc, skip next 3 sc, sc in next 7 sc, ★ skip next 3 sc, 7 dc in next sc, skip next 3 sc, sc in next 7 sc; repeat from ★ across to last 4 sc, skip next 3 sc, 4 dc in last sc.

Rows 6-80: Repeat Rows 2-5, 18 times; then repeat Rows 2-4 once **more**; at end of Row 80, change to Rose Ombre in last sc made *(Fig. 7b, page 140)*.

SHOPPING LIST

Yarn
(Medium Weight)
[4 ounces, 204 yards
(113 grams, 186 meters)
per skein]:
☐ Teal Ombre - 5 skeins
☐ Green Ombre - 1 skein
☐ Rose Ombre - 1 skein

Crochet Hook
☐ Size I (5.5 mm)
or size needed for gauge

Additional Supplies
☐ Yarn needle

Edging

Rnd 1: Ch 2 **(counts as first hdc, now and throughout)**, turn; hdc in next sc and in each sc across, ch 1; working in ends of rows, hdc in first 3 sc rows, 3 hdc in next dc row, (hdc in next 3 sc rows, 3 hdc in next dc row) across, ch 1; working over chs and in free loops of beginning ch *(Fig. 6b, page 140)*, hdc in first ch, ★ 3 hdc in next sp, hdc in next 7 chs, 3 hdc in next sp, hdc in next ch; repeat from ★ across, ch 1; working in ends of rows, 3 hdc in first dc row, (hdc in next 3 sc rows, 3 hdc in next dc row) across; ch 1, cut Teal Ombre; join with slip st to first hdc changing to Green Ombre *(Fig. 7c, page 140)*: 522 hdc and 4 corner ch-1 sps.

Rnd 2: Ch 2, do **not** turn; 2 hdc in next hdc and in each hdc and each corner ch-1 sp around; join with slip st to first hdc, finish off.

Lily Pad (Make 7)

With Green Ombre, ch 3; join with slip st to form a ring.

Row 1 (Right side): Ch 3, 12 dc in ring; do **not** join: 13 dc.

Note: Mark Row 1 as **right** side.

Row 2: Ch 3, turn; dc in first dc, 2 dc in each of next 5 dc, 3 dc in next dc, 2 dc in each of last 6 dc: 27 dc.

Row 3: Ch 3, turn; dc in first 3 dc, 2 dc in next dc, dc in next dc, hdc in next 4 dc, sc in next 4 dc, 3 hdc in next dc, sc in next 4 dc, hdc in next 4 dc, dc in next dc, 2 dc in next dc, dc in next 2 dc, 2 dc in last dc; finish off leaving a long end for sewing.

Lily (Make 3)

With Rose Ombre, ch 3; join with slip st to form a ring.

Rnd 1 (Right side): Ch 2, 12 dc in ring; join with slip st to first dc: 12 dc.

Note: Mark Rnd 1 as **right** side.

Begin working in rows.

Row 1: Ch 3, do **not** turn; 3 dc in same st as joining, 2 dc in each of next 7 dc, 4 dc in next dc, leave remaining 3 dc unworked: 22 dc.

Row 2: Ch 3, turn; hdc in first dc, sc in next 7 dc, hdc in next 6 dc, sc in next 7 dc, hdc in last dc; finish off leaving a long end for sewing.

Using photo as a guide for placement and long ends, sew **wrong** side of Lily Pads and Lilies to right side of Blanket.

HAT

With Teal Ombre, ch 3; join with slip st to form a ring.

Rnd 1 (Right side)**:** Ch 3 **(does not count as a st, now and throughout)**, 12 dc in ring; skip beginning ch-3 **(now and throughout)** and join with slip st to first dc.

Rnd 2: Ch 3, 2 dc in same st as joining and in each dc around; join with slip st to first dc: 24 dc.

Rnd 3: Ch 3, dc in same st as joining, 2 dc in next dc, (dc in next dc, 2 dc in next dc) around; join with slip st to first dc: 36 dc.

Rnd 4: Ch 3, dc in same st as joining and in next dc, 2 dc in next dc, (dc in next 2 dc, 2 dc in next dc) around; join with slip st to first dc: 48 dc.

Rnd 5: Ch 3, dc in same st as joining and in next 2 dc, 2 dc in next dc, (dc in next 3 dc, 2 dc in next dc) around; join with slip st to first dc: 60 dc.

SIZE 0-6 MONTHS ONLY

Rnd 6: Ch 3, dc in same st as joining and in each dc around; join with slip st to first dc.

SIZE 6-12 MONTHS ONLY

Rnd 6: Ch 3, dc in same st as joining and in next 8 dc, 2 dc in next dc, (dc in next 9 dc, 2 dc in next dc) around; join with slip st to first dc: 66 dc.

Rnd 7: Ch 3, dc in same st as joining and in each dc around; join with slip st to first dc.

BOTH SIZES

Rnd 7{8}: Ch 3, dc in same st as joining and in each dc around, cut Teal Ombre; join with slip st to first dc changing to Green Ombre *(Fig. 7a, page 140)*.

Rnd 8{9}: Ch 3, dc in same st as joining and in each dc around; join with slip st to first dc.

Rnd 9{10}: Ch 3, dc in same st as joining and in each dc around, cut Green Ombre; join with slip st to first dc changing to Rose Ombre.

Last 2 Rnds: Ch 2 **(does not count as a st)**, hdc in same st as joining and in each st around; skip beginning ch-2 and join with slip st to first hdc.

Finish off.

Design by Sara Leighton.

ASHLEY DRESS

EASY

SIZE: 12 TO 18 MONTHS

GAUGE INFORMATION

In Yoke pattern,
   18 dc = 4" (10 cm)
   Rnds 1-10 = 3¾" (9.5 cm)
In Skirt pattern,
   (dc, ch 2, dc) 6 times and
   8 rnds = 3" (7.5 cm)

Gauge Swatch: 4"(10 cm) square
Ch 20.
Row 1: Dc in fourth ch from hook **(3 skipped chs count as first dc)** and in each ch across: 18 dc.
Rows 2-8: Ch 3 **(counts as first dc)**, turn; dc in next dc and in each dc across. Finish off.

STITCH GUIDE

TREBLE CROCHET *(abbreviated tr)*
YO twice, insert hook in sc indicated, YO and pull up a loop (4 loops on hook), (YO and draw through 2 loops on hook) 3 times.

YOKE

Foundation Rnd: With Tan, ch 4, YO, insert hook in fourth ch from hook **(3 skipped chs count as first fdc)**, YO and pull up a loop (3 loops on hook), YO and draw through one loop on hook **(ch made)**, (YO and draw through 2 loops on hook) twice **(fdc made)**, work fdc for a total of 72 sts *(see Foundation Double Crochet, page 139)*; join with slip st to first fdc.

Rnd 1 (Right side): Ch 3, dc in next 2 fdc, 2 dc in next fdc, dc in next 4 fdc, 2 dc in next fdc, ★ dc in next 3 fdc, 2 dc in next fdc, dc in next 4 fdc, 2 dc in next fdc; repeat from ★ around; join with slip st to first dc: 88 dc.

Note: Loop a short piece of yarn around any stitch to mark Rnd 1 as **right** side.

Rnd 2: Ch 1, sc in same st as joining, tr in next dc, (sc in next dc, tr in next dc) around; join with slip st to first sc.

Rnd 3: Ch 3, dc in next 3 sts, 2 dc in next sc, dc in next 5 sts, 2 dc in next sc, ★ dc in next 4 sts, 2 dc in next st, dc in next 5 sts, 2 dc in next st; repeat from ★ around; join with slip st to first dc: 104 dc.

SHOPPING LIST

Yarn
(Light Weight)
[5 ounces, 362 yards
(140 grams, 331 meters)
per skein]:

☐ Tan - 1 skein
☐ Peach - 1 skein
☐ Variegated - 1 skein
☐ Rose - 40 yards (36.5 meters)
☐ Tan - 20 yards (18.5 meters)

Crochet Hook
☐ Size G (4 mm)
   or size needed for gauge

ASHLEY DRESS

Rnd 4: Ch 1, sc in same st as joining, tr in next dc, (sc in next dc, tr in next dc) around; join with slip st to first sc.

Rnd 5: Ch 3, dc in next 4 sts, 2 dc in next tr, dc in next 6 sts, 2 dc in next sc, ★ dc in next 5 sts, 2 dc in next st, dc in next 6 sts, 2 dc in next st; repeat from ★ around; join with slip st to first dc: 120 dc.

Rnd 6: Ch 1, sc in same st as joining, tr in next dc, (sc in next dc, tr in next dc) around; join with slip st to first sc.

Rnd 7: Ch 3, dc in next 5 sts, 2 dc in next st, dc in next 7 sts, 2 dc in next st, ★ dc in next 6 sts, 2 dc in next st, dc in next 7 sts, 2 dc in next st; repeat from ★ around; join with slip st to first dc: 136 dc.

Rnd 8: Ch 1, sc in same st as joining, tr in next dc, (sc in next dc, tr in next dc) around; join with slip st to first sc.

Rnd 9: Ch 3, dc in next 4 sts, 2 dc in next st, ★ (dc in next 6 sts, 2 dc in next st) 5 times, dc in next 5 sts, 2 dc in next st; repeat from ★ around to last 7 sts, dc in next 6 sts, 2 dc in last tr; join with slip st to first dc: 156 dc.

Rnd 10: Ch 1, sc in same st as joining, tr in next dc, (sc in next dc, tr in next dc) around; join with slip st to first sc; do not finish off.

SKIRT

Rnd 1: Ch 3, dc in next 20 sts, ch 2, skip next 36 sts (**armhole**), dc in next 42 sts, ch 2, skip next 36 sts (**armhole**), dc in last 21 sts; join with slip st to first dc: 84 dc and 4 chs.

Rnd 2: Ch 2, turn; hdc in next 21 dc, hdc in next 2 chs, hdc in next 42 dc, hdc in next 2 chs, hdc in last 20 hdc; join with slip st to Back Loop Only of first hdc *(Fig. 5, page 140)*: 88 hdc.

Rnd 3: Ch 2, turn; working from left to right, work reverse sc in Front Loop Only of each hdc around *(Figs. 12a-d, page 141)*; join with slip st to first st.

Rnd 4: Ch 1, do **not** turn; working in free loops on Rnd 2 *(Fig. 6a, page 140)*, (dc, ch 1, dc) in first hdc, skip next hdc, ★ (dc, ch 1, dc) in next hdc, skip next hdc; repeat from ★ around; join with slip st to first dc: 88 dc and 44 ch-1 sps.

Rnds 5-7: Slip st in first ch-1 sp, ch 4 (**counts as first dc plus ch 1, now and throughout**), dc in same sp, (dc, ch 1, dc) in next ch-1 sp and in each ch-1 sp around; join with slip st to first dc.

Finish off.

Rnd 8: With **right** side facing, join Peach in first ch-1 sp *(see Joining With Dc, page 139)*; ch 1, dc in same sp, (dc, ch 1, dc) in next ch-1 sp and in each ch-1 sp around; join with slip st to first dc.

Rnds 9-15: Slip st in first ch-1 sp, ch 4, dc in same sp, (dc, ch 1, dc) in next ch-1 sp and in each ch-1 sp around; join with slip st to first dc.

Finish off.

Rnd 16: With **right** side facing, join Variegated with dc in first ch-1 sp; ch 2, dc in same sp, (dc, ch 2, dc) in next ch-1 sp and in each ch-1 sp around; join with slip st to first dc: 88 dc and 44 ch-2 sps.

Rnds 17-22: Slip st in first ch-2 sp, ch 5 (**counts as first dc plus ch 2**), dc in same sp, (dc, ch 2, dc) in next ch-2 sp and in each ch-2 sp around; join with slip st to first dc.

Finish off.

Rnd 23: With **right** side facing, join Rose with dc in first ch-2 sp; ch 3, dc in same sp, (dc, ch 3, dc) in next ch-2 sp and in each ch-2 sp around; join with slip st to first dc: 44 ch-3 sps.

Rnd 24: (Slip st, 5 sc) in first ch-3 sp, 5 sc in next ch-3 sp and in each ch-3 sp around; join with slip st to first sc, finish off.

Rnd 25: With right side facing, working **behind** Rnd 24 *(Fig. 9, page 141)* and in skipped dc on Rnd 23, join White with dc in last dc; ch 3, dc in third ch from hook, dc in next dc, ★ dc in next dc, ch 3, dc in third ch from hook, dc in next dc; repeat from ★ around; join with slip st to first dc, finish off.

Design by Lois J. Long

FOX BIB

 EASY

Finished Size: 7½" wide x 8" long, (19 cm x 20.5 cm)

GAUGE INFORMATION
11 sc and 12.5 rows = 3" (7.5 cm)
Gauge Swatch: 3" wide x 2⅞" high (7.5 cm x 7.25 cm)
With Red, ch 12.
Row 1: Sc in second ch from hook and in each ch across: 11 sc.
Rows 2-12: Ch 1, turn; sc in each sc across.
Finish off.

STITCH GUIDE
SINGLE CROCHET 2 TOGETHER
(abbreviated sc2tog)
Pull up a loop in each of next 2 sc, YO and draw through all 3 loops on hook (**counts as one sc**).

HEAD
With Red and beginning at top of Head, ch 26.

Row 1 (Right side)**:** Sc in second ch from hook and in each ch across: 25 sc.

Note: Loop a short piece of yarn around any stitch to mark Row 1 as **right** side.

Rows 2-13: Ch 1, turn; sc in each sc across.

Row 14: Ch 1, turn; sc in each sc across changing to Black in last sc *(Fig. 7b, page 140)*; cut Red.

Row 15: Ch 1, turn; sc in first sc, skip next sc, sc in next 10 sc, 3 sc in next sc, sc in next 10 sc, skip next sc, sc in last sc.

Row 16: Ch 1, turn; sc in first sc, skip next sc, sc in next 10 sc, 3 sc in next sc, sc in next 10 sc, skip next sc, sc in last sc changing to Off White; cut Black.

Rows 17-24: Ch 1, turn; sc in first sc, skip next sc, sc in next 10 sc, 3 sc in next sc, sc in next 10 sc, skip next sc, sc in last sc.

SHOPPING LIST

Yarn
(Medium Weight) [4]
[1.75 ounces, 80 yards (50 grams, 73 meters) per ball]:
☐ Red - 40 yards (36.5 meters)
☐ Off White - 25 yards (23 meters)
☐ Black - 15 yards (13.5 meters)

Crochet Hook
☐ Size G (4 mm)
or size needed for gauge

Additional Supplies
☐ Yarn needle

Edging: Ch 1, turn; sc in first sc, skip next sc, sc in next 10 sc, 3 sc in next sc, sc in next 10 sc, skip next sc, sc in last sc; sc evenly across end of rows; working in free loops of beginning ch *(Fig. 6b, page 140)*, sc in first 4 chs, place marker in last sc made for Tie placement, sc in next 17 chs, place marker in last sc made for Tie placement, sc in next 4 chs; sc evenly across end of rows; join with slip st to first sc, finish off.

Tie

With **right** side facing, join Red with slip st in either marked sc on Edging, remove marker; ch 52, hdc in back ridge of second ch from hook *(Fig. 4, page 140)* and each ch across; slip st in next sc on Edging, finish off.

Repeat for second Tie in remaining marked sc.

FEATURES

Ear (Make 2)
With Black, ch 2.

Row 1 (Right side): 2 Sc in second ch from hook.

Note: Mark Row 1 as **right** side.

Row 2: Ch 1, turn; 2 sc in each sc across: 4 sc.

Row 3: Ch 1, turn; 2 sc in first sc, sc in next 2 sc, 2 sc in last sc: 6 sc.

Rows 4-6: Ch 1, turn; sc in each sc across.

Row 7: Ch 1, turn; beginning in first sc, sc2tog, sc in next 2 sc, sc2tog; finish off leaving a long end for sewing: 4 sc.

Eye (Make 2)
OUTER
With Off White, ch 2.

Rnd 1 (Right side): 7 Sc in second ch from hook; join with slip st to first sc.

Note: Mark Rnd 1 as **right** side.

Rnd 2: Ch 1, 2 sc in same st as joining and in each sc around; join with slip st to first sc, finish off leaving a long end for sewing.

CENTER
With Black, ch 2.

Rnd 1 (Right side): 6 Sc in second ch from hook; join with slip st to first sc, finish off leaving a long end for sewing.

Sew **wrong** side of Center to **right** side of Outer Eye; then add eyelashes using straight stitches *(Fig. 18, page 143)*.

FINISHING

Using photo as a guide for placement and with **right** side of all pieces facing:
Sew Ears and Eyes to Head.
Using a double strand of Black, add a backstitch mouth *(Fig. 17, page 143)* and a satin stitch nose *(Figs. 19a & b, page 143)*.

Design by Kristi Simpson.

DOLL

EASY

Finished Size: Approximately 9" (23 cm) tall
Blanket instructions on page 14.

GAUGE INFORMATION
Gauge for the doll is not of great importance as long as your crochet fabric is very dense.

STITCH GUIDE

SINGLE CROCHET 2 TOGETHER
(abbreviated sc2tog)
Pull up a loop in each of next 2 sc, YO and draw through all 3 loops on hook **(counts as one sc)**.

HEAD

Rnd 1 (Right side): With Skin color, make an adjustable loop to form a ring *(Figs. 3a-d, page 139)*; work 6 sc in ring; do **not** join, place marker to indicate beginning of rnd *(see Markers, page 140)*.

Rnd 2: 2 Sc in each sc around: 12 sc.

Rnd 3: (Sc in next sc, 2 sc in next sc) around: 18 sc.

Rnd 4: (Sc in next 2 sc, 2 sc in next sc) around: 24 sc.

Rnd 5: (Sc in next 3 sc, 2 sc in next sc) around: 30 sc.

Rnd 6: (Sc in next 4 sc, 2 sc in next sc) around: 36 sc.

Rnd 7: (Sc in next 5 sc, 2 sc in next sc) around: 42 sc.

Rnd 8: (Sc in next 6 sc, 2 sc in next sc) around: 48 sc.

Rnd 9: (Sc in next 7 sc, 2 sc in next sc) around: 54 sc.

Rnds 10-15: Sc in each sc around.

Rnd 16: (Sc in next 7 sc, sc2tog) around: 48 sc.

Rnd 17: (Sc in next 6 sc, sc2tog) around: 42 sc.

Rnd 18: (Sc in next 5 sc, sc2tog) around: 36 sc.

Rnd 19: (Sc in next 4 sc, sc2tog) around: 30 sc.

Rnd 20: (Sc in next 3 sc, sc2tog) around: 24 sc.

SHOPPING LIST

Yarn
(Light Weight)
☐ Grey - 130 yards (119 meters)
(Medium Weight)
☐ Skin color - 60 yards (55 meters)
☐ Pink - 6 yards (5.5 meters)

Crochet Hook
☐ Size E (3.5 mm)

Additional Supplies
☐ Safety pin - for optional marker
☐ Brown embroidery floss
☐ Pink embroidery floss
☐ Yarn and tapestry needles
☐ Polyester fiberfill

DOLL

Rnd 21: (Sc in next 2 sc, sc2tog) around: 18 sc.

Stuff Head with polyester fiberfill.

Rnd 22: (Sc in next sc, sc2tog) around: 12 sc.

Rnd 23: Sc2tog around; slip st in next sc, finish off leaving a long end for sewing: 6 sc.

HAT

Rnd 1 (Right side): With Grey, make an adjustable loop to form a ring; work 6 sc in ring; do **not** join, place marker.

Rnd 2: 2 Sc in each sc around: 12 sc.

Rnd 3: (Hdc in next sc, 2 hdc in next sc) around: 18 hdc.

Rnd 4: (Hdc in next 2 hdc, 2 hdc in next hdc) around: 24 hdc.

Rnd 5: (Hdc in next 3 hdc, 2 hdc in next hdc) around: 30 hdc.

Rnd 6: (Hdc in next 4 hdc, 2 hdc in next hdc) around: 36 hdc.

Rnd 7: (Hdc in next 5 hdc, 2 hdc in next hdc) around: 42 hdc.

Rnds 8-10: Hdc in each hdc around.

Rnd 11: Hdc in each hdc around changing to Pink in last hdc *(Fig. 7c, page 140)*; cut Grey.

Rnd 12: Sc in each hdc around; slip st in next sc, finish off leaving a long end for sewing.

HEAD ASSEMBLY

Use photos as guides for placement of all pieces.

Use whipstitch *(Figs. 13d & e, page 142)* for the method of sewing to join the pieces together.

Sew the Hat to the Head, placing it at an angle.

Insert the yarn ends through the Head and out the beginning ring where it will be attached to the Body; do **not** cut yarn.

With Pink embroidery floss, insert needle in at the bottom of the Head and back out on Rnd 7. Embroider mouth using satin stitch *(Fig. 19b, page 143)*.
Finish by pushing the needle back through the Head and out near the other yarn end. Knot the two ends together, then hide the ends.

With Skin color, embroider nose on Rnds 9 and 10 in same manner.

With Brown embroidery floss, embroider eyes on Rnd 11, 7 sc apart in same manner.

FIRST LEG

Rnd 1 (Right side): With Grey, make an adjustable loop to form a ring; work 6 sc in ring; do **not** join, place marker.

Rnd 2: 2 Sc in each sc around: 12 sc.

Rnd 3: (Sc in next sc, 2 sc in next sc) around: 18 sc.

Rnd 4: (Sc in next 2 sc, 2 sc in next sc) around: 24 sc.

Rnd 5: Sc in next 14 sc, sc2tog, (sc in next 2 sc, sc2tog) twice: 21 sc.

Rnd 6: Sc in next 15 sc, sc2tog 3 times: 18 sc.

Rnd 7: Sc in next 14 sc, sc2tog twice: 16 sc.

Rnds 8-13: Sc in each sc around.

Rnd 14: Sc in next 6 sc, sc2tog twice, sc in next 6 sc: 14 sc.

Rnd 15: Sc in each sc around.

Rnd 16: (2 Sc in next sc, sc in next 6 sc) twice: 16 sc.

Rnds 17-19: Sc in each sc around.

Slip st in next sc, finish off leaving a long end for sewing.

SECOND LEG

Work same as First Leg through Rnd 18: 16 sc.

Joining: Sc in next 6 sc, working in next sc and in same sc as slip st on First Leg, sc2tog, sc in next 7 sc; remove marker and place marker here to indicate the new beginning of rnd; do **not** finish off.

BODY

Rnd 1: Sc in next 7 sc, working in last sc on same Leg and in next sc on next Leg, sc2tog, sc in each sc around: 30 sc.

Rnd 2: (Sc in next 3 sc, 2 sc in next sc) 3 times, sc in each sc around: 33 sc.

Rnd 3: (Sc in next 4 sc, 2 sc in next sc) 3 times, sc in each sc around: 36 sc.

Rnds 4-6: Sc in each sc around.

Rnd 7: (Sc in next 4 sc, sc2tog) 3 times, sc in each sc around: 33 sc.

Rnd 8: Sc in next 6 sc, sc2tog, (sc in next sc, sc2tog) twice, sc in each sc around: 30 sc.

Rnds 9-13: Sc in each sc around.

Stuff Legs and Body with polyester fiberfill as you work.

Rnd 14: (Sc in next 3 sc, sc2tog) around: 24 sc.

Rnds 15 and 16: Sc in each sc around.

Rnd 17: (Sc in next 2 sc, sc2tog) around: 18 sc.

Rnds 18-20: Sc in each sc around.

Rnd 21: Sc2tog around: 9 sc.

Continue to decrease around until hole is closed; slip st in next sc, finish off leaving a long end.

ARM (Make 2)

Rnd 1 (Right side): With Skin color, make an adjustable loop to form a ring; work 6 sc in ring; do **not** join, place marker.

Rnd 2: 2 Sc in each sc around: 12 sc.

Rnd 3: (Sc in next sc, 2 sc in next sc) around: 18 sc.

Rnd 4: (Sc in next 4 sc, sc2tog) around: 15 sc.

Rnd 5: (Sc in next 3 sc, sc2tog) around changing to Pink in last sc *(Fig. 7e, page 140)*; cut Skin color: 12 sc.

Rnd 6: Sc in each sc around changing to Grey in last sc; cut Pink.

Rnd 7: (Sc in next sc, 2 sc in next sc) around: 18 sc.

Stuff Arm with polyester fiberfill as you work.

Rnds 8-13: Sc in each sc around.

Rnd 14: (Sc in next 4 sc, sc2tog) around: 15 sc.

Rnds 15 and 16: Sc in each sc around.

Rnd 17: (Sc in next 3 sc, sc2tog) around: 12 sc.

Rnds 18 and 19: Sc in each sc around.

Slip st in next sc, finish off leaving a long end for sewing.

BODY ASSEMBLY

Flatten last rnd of Arms and sew closed. Sew Arms to Body on the third rnd from the top. Insert the yarn ends through the Body and out the neck; do not cut yarn.

Tie all strands together at the neck, then hide all yarn ends in the Body.

Sew Head to Body, sewing around the neck 3 times; secure and hide yarn end.

Design by Tamara Ramsey.

DENIM DIAPER COVER

 EASY

SIZE INFORMATION
Finished Measurements:

Size	Waist	Rise (from top of front to top of back)
0-3 Months	12½" (32 cm)	13" (33 cm)
3-6 Months	13¾" (35 cm)	15" (38 cm)
6-12 Months	15" (38 cm)	16½" (42 cm)

Size Note: We have printed the instructions for the sizes in different colors to make it easier for you to find:
- Size 0-3 months in Blue
- Size 3-6 months in Pink
- Size 6-12 months in Green

Instructions in Black apply to all sizes.

GAUGE INFORMATION
14 sc and 16 rows = 4" (10 cm)
In (sc, dc) pattern,
　14 sts and 12 rows = 4" (10 cm)
Gauge Swatch: 4" (10 cm) square
With Blue, ch 15.
Row 1: Sc in second ch from hook and in each ch across: 14 sc.
Rows 2-16: Ch 1, turn; sc in each sc across.
Finish off.

STITCH GUIDE
SINGLE CROCHET 2 TOGETHER
　(abbreviated sc2tog)
Pull up a loop in each of next 2 sts, YO and draw through all 3 loops on hook **(counts as one sc)**.

FRONT POST TREBLE CROCHET
　(abbreviated FPtr)
YO twice, working in **front** of previous row, insert hook from **front** to **back** around post of st indicated *(Fig. 10, page 141)*, YO and pull up a loop (4 loops on hook), (YO and draw through 2 loops on hook) 3 times.

BODY
With Blue and leaving a long end for sewing, ch 23{25-27}.

Row 1 (Right side): Sc in second ch from hook and in each ch across: 22{24-26} sc.

Note: Loop a short piece of yarn around any stitch to mark Row 1 as **right** side.

SHOPPING LIST

Yarn
(Medium Weight) 4
[5 ounces, 251 yards (142 grams, 230 meters) per skein]:
☐ Blue - 1 skein
☐ Gold - 40 yards (36.5 meters)

Crochet Hook
☐ Size J (6 mm)
　or size needed for gauge

Additional Supplies
☐ Yarn needle

113

DENIM DIAPER COVER

Rows 2 thru 11{12-14}: Ch 1, turn; sc in first st, dc in next st, (sc in next st, dc in next st) across.

Rows 12{13-15} thru 16{17-19} (Decrease rows): Ch 1, turn; sc in first st, sc2tog, sc in each st across to last 3 sts, sc2tog, sc in last st: 12{14-16} sc.

Rows 17{18-20} thru 28{33-37}: Ch 1, turn; sc in each sc across.

Rows 29{34-38} thru 33{38-42} (Increase rows): Ch 1, turn; 2 sc in first sc, sc in each sc across to last sc, 2 sc in last sc: 22{24-26} sc.

Rows 34{39-43} thru 43{49-55}: Ch 1, turn; sc in first st, (dc in next st, sc in next st) across.

Row 44{50-56}: Ch 1, turn; sc in each st across; finish off leaving a long end for sewing.

Using long end and matching rows, use mattress stitch *(Figs. 14a & b, page 142)* to join first and last 11{12-14} rows together on **each** side.

BELT LOOPS

Rnd 1: With **right** side facing, join Gold with sc in first sc on Body; sc in next 2 sc, work FPtr around st **below** next st, (sc in next 3 sts, work FPtr around st **below** next st) around working in sts and in free loop of each beginning ch *(Fig. 6b, page 140)*; join with slip st to first sc, finish off: 44{48-52} sts.

LEG EDGING

Rnd 1: With **right** side facing, join Gold with sc at seam on Leg opening; sc evenly around; join with slip st to first sc, finish off.

Rnd 2: With right side facing, join Blue with sc in first sc; sc in each sc around; join with slip st to first sc, finish off.

Repeat for second Leg.

POCKET (Make 2)

With Gold and leaving a long end for sewing, ch 9.

Row 1 (Right side): Sc in second ch from hook and in each ch across: 8 sc.

Row 2: Ch 1, turn; sc in each sc across.

Row 3: Ch 1, turn; sc in Back Loop Only of each sc across *(Fig. 5, page 140)*.

Rows 4-6: Ch 1, turn; sc in both loops of each sc across.

Row 7: Ch 1, turn; beginning in first sc, sc2tog 4 times: 4 sc.

Row 8: Ch 1, turn; beginning in first sc, sc2tog twice: 2 sc.

Row 9: Ch 1, turn; beginning in first sc, sc2tog; finish off.

Using photo as a guide for placement and long end, sew Pockets to Diaper Cover.

Design by Kristi Simpson.

CAT BOTTLE COVER

 EASY

Finished Size: Fits an 8 ounce bottle

GAUGE INFORMATION
Gauge Swatch: 2" (5 cm) diameter
With larger size hook, work same as Cover for 4 rnds: 24 sc.

STITCH GUIDE
TREBLE CROCHET *(abbreviated tr)*
YO twice, insert hook in st indicated, YO and pull up a loop (4 loops on hook), (YO and draw through 2 loops on hook) 3 times.

COVER
With larger size hook and White, ch 4; join with slip st to form a ring.

Rnd 1 (Right side)**:** 2 Sc in same st and in each ch around; do **not** join, place marker to indicated beginning of rnd *(see Markers, page 140)*: 8 sc.

Rnd 2: 2 Sc in each sc around: 16 sc.

Rnd 3: (Sc in next sc, 2 sc in next sc) around: 24 sc.

Rnds 4-14: Sc in each sc around.

Rnd 15: (Ch 1, sc in next sc) around.

Rnd 16: (Skip next ch-1 sp, sc in next sc) around.

Rnds 17-25: Repeat Rnds 15 and 16, 4 times; then repeat Rnd 15 once **more**.

Finish off.

HEAD
With smaller size hook and White, ch 4; join with slip st to form a ring.

Rnd 1: Sc in same st, 2 sc in next ch, sc in next ch, 2 sc in next ch; do **not** join, place marker: 6 sc.

Rnd 2: Sc in next sc, 2 sc in next sc, sc in next 2 sc, 2 sc in next sc, sc in next sc: 8 sc.

SHOPPING LIST

Yarn
(Medium Weight) 4
☐ White - 85 yards (77.5 meters)
☐ Black - small amount
☐ Pink - small amount
☐ Blue - small amount

Crochet Hook
☐ Size F (3.75 mm) **and**
☐ Size G (4 mm)
 or size needed for gauge

Additional Supplies
☐ Polyester stuffing
☐ ½" Ribbon - 15" (43 cm)
☐ Yarn needle

Rnd 3: Sc in next 3 sc, 2 sc in each of next 2 sc, sc in next 3 sc: 10 sc.

Rnd 4: (Sc in next 2 sc, 2 sc in each of next 2 sc) twice, sc in next 2 sc: 14 sc.

Rnd 5: Sc in next 2 sc, 2 sc in each of next 2 sc, sc in next 6 sc, 2 sc in each of next 2 sc, sc in next 2 sc: 18 sc.

Rnd 6: Sc in next 9 sc, 5 sc in next sc, sc in each sc around: 22 sc.

Rnd 7: Sc in each sc around.

Rnd 8: Sc in next 9 sc, 2 sc in next sc, sc in next 4 sc, 2 sc in next sc, sc in each sc around: 24 sc.

Rnd 9: Sc in next 6 sc, 2 sc in next sc, sc in next 12 sc, 2 sc in next sc, sc in each sc around: 26 sc.

Rnd 10 (Ears): Sc in next 9 sc, working in Front Loops Only *(Fig. 5, page 140)*, slip st in next sc, † hdc in next sc, (dc, tr, ch 2, slip st in second ch from hook, tr, dc) in next sc, hdc in next sc †, slip st in next 2 sc, repeat from † to † once, slip st in next sc, sc in **both** loops of each sc around.

Rnd 11: Sc in next 9 sc, sc in free loops of next 10 sc **behind** Ears *(Fig. 9, page 141)*, sc in **both** loops of each sc around.

Rnd 12: (Skip next sc, sc in next sc) twice, (skip next sc, sc in next 2 sc) 6 times, (skip next sc, sc in next sc) twice: 16 sc.

Stuff Head lightly with polyester fiberfill.

Rnd 13: (Skip next sc, sc in next sc) around: 8 sc.

Rnd 14: (Skip next sc, sc in next sc) around; finish off leaving a long end for sewing.

ARM (Make 2)

With smaller size hook and White, ch 4; join with slip st to form a ring.

Rnd 1 (Right side): 2 Sc in same st and in each ch around; do **not** join, place marker: 8 sc.

Rnd 2: (Sc in next sc, 2 sc in next sc) around: 12 sc.

Rnd 3: Sc in each sc around.

Rnd 4: (Skip next sc, sc in next sc) 4 times, sc in next 4 sc: 8 sc.

Rnds 5-10: Sc in each sc around.

Rnd 11: (Skip next sc, slip st in next sc) around; finish off leavinf a long end for sewing.

Flatten Arm.

LEG (Make 2)

With smaller size hook and White, ch 4; join with slip st to form a ring.

Rnd 1 (Right side): 2 Sc in same st and in each ch around; do **not** join, place marker: 8 sc.

Rnd 2: (Sc in next sc, 2 sc in next sc) around: 12 sc.

Rnds 3 and 4: Sc in each sc around.

Rnd 5: (Skip next sc, sc in next sc) 4 times, sc in next 4 sc: 8 sc.

Stuff Leg lightly with polyester fiberfill.

Rnds 6-11: Sc in each sc around.

Rnd 12: (Skip next sc, slip st in next sc) around; finish off leaving a long end for sewing.

FINISHING

Using photo as a guide for placement: Sew Arms and Legs to Cover.

Using Embroidery Stitches on page 143, add facial features to Head.

Tie ribbon in a bow around neck.

Design by Sue Penrod.

CABLES CAR SEAT COVER

 EASY

Finished Size: 33" x 36½" (84 cm x 92.5 cm)

GAUGE INFORMATION

In pattern,
one repeat (10 sts) = 3" (7.5 cm);
8 rows = 3¼" (8.25 cm)

Gauge Swatch: 5½" wide x 4" high
(14 cm x 10 cm)

Ch 19.

Work same as Body for 10 rows:
18 hdc.

Finish off.

STITCH GUIDE

FRONT POST TREBLE CROCHET
(abbreviated FPtr)

YO twice, insert hook from **front** to **back** around post of st indicated *(Fig. 10, page 141)*, YO and pull up a loop even with loops on hook (4 loops on hook), (YO and draw through 2 loops on hook) 3 times. Skip hdc **behind** FPtr.

FRONT POST DOUBLE TREBLE CROCHET *(abbreviated FPdtr)*

YO 3 times, insert hook from **front** to **back** around post of st indicated *(Fig. 10, page 141)*, YO and pull up a loop even with loops on hook (5 loops on hook), (YO and draw through 2 loops on hook) 4 times. Skip hdc **behind** FPdtr.

BODY

Ch 109.

Row 1 (Right side)**:** Hdc in third ch from hook **(2 skipped chs count as first hdc, now and throughout)** and in each ch across: 108 hdc.

Note: Loop a short piece of yarn around any stitch to mark Row 1 as **right** side **and** bottom edge.

Row 2: Ch 2 **(counts as first hdc, now and throughout)**, turn; hdc in next hdc and in each hdc across.

Row 3: Ch 2, turn; hdc in next hdc, skip next 2 hdc 2 rows **below**, work FPdtr around each of next 2 hdc 2 rows **below**, working in **front** of last 2 FPdtr made, work FPdtr around each of 2 skipped hdc, hdc in next 2 hdc, ★ work FPtr around each of next 2 hdc 2 rows **below**, hdc in next 2 hdc, skip next 2 hdc 2 rows **below**, work FPdtr around each of next 2 hdc 2 rows **below**, working in **front** of last 2 FPdtr made, work FPdtr around each of 2 skipped hdc, hdc in next 2 hdc; repeat from ★ across.

SHOPPING LIST

Yarn
(Light Weight)
[3.5 ounces, 254 yards
(100 grams, 232 meters)
per skein]:
☐ 6 skeins

Crochet Hook
☐ Size I (5.5 mm)
   or size needed for gauge

Additional Supplies
☐ Tapestry needle
☐ ¹³⁄₁₆" (20 mm) Buttons

CABLES CAR SEAT COVER

Row 4: Ch 2, turn; hdc in next st and in each st across.

Row 5: Ch 2, turn; hdc in next hdc, work FPtr around each of next 4 FPdtr 2 rows **below**, hdc in next 2 hdc, ★ work FPtr around each of next 2 FPtr 2 rows **below**, hdc in next 2 hdc, work FPtr around each of next 4 FPdtr 2 rows **below**, hdc in next 2 hdc; repeat from ★ across.

Row 6: Ch 2, turn; hdc in next st and in each st across.

Row 7: Ch 2, turn; hdc in next hdc, skip next 2 FPtr 2 rows **below**, work FPdtr around each of next 2 FPtr 2 rows **below**, working in **front** of last 2 FPdtr made, work FPdtr around each of 2 skipped FPtr, hdc in next 2 hdc, ★ work FPtr around each of next 2 FPtr 2 rows **below**, hdc in next 2 hdc, skip next 2 FPtr 2 rows **below**, work FPdtr around each of next 2 FPtr 2 rows **below**, working in **front** of last 2 FPdtr made, work FPdtr around each of 2 skipped FPtr, hdc in next 2 hdc; repeat from ★ across.

Repeat Rows 4-7 for pattern until piece measures approximately 36" (91.5 cm) from beginning ch, ending by working a right side row; do **not** finish off.

EDGING

Rnd 1: Ch 1, do **not** turn; sc evenly around entire Body working 3 sc in each corner; join with slip st to first sc.

Rnd 2: Ch 1; working from **left** to **right**, work reverse sc in each sc around *(Figs. 12a-d, page 141)*; join with slip st to first st, finish off.

BUTTONHOLE STRAP
(Make 2)
Ch 11.

Row 1 (Right side)**:** Working in back ridge of beginning ch *(Fig. 4, page 140)*, hdc in third ch from hook and each ch across: 10 hdc.

Row 2: Ch 2, turn; hdc in next hdc and in each hdc across.

Row 3 (Buttonhole row)**:** Ch 2, turn; hdc in next 3 hdc, ch 2, skip next 2 hdc, hdc in last 4 hdc: 8 hdc and one ch-2 sp.

Row 4: Ch 2, turn; hdc in next 3 hdc, 2 hdc in next ch-2 sp, hdc in last 4 hdc: 10 hdc.

Row 5: Ch 2, turn; hdc in next hdc and in each hdc across.

Repeat Row 5 until Strap measures approximately 7" (18 cm) from beginning ch.

Finish off leaving a long end for sewing.

Sew last row of each Strap approximately 8" (20.5 cm) from top edge of Body and 11" (28 cm) from each side edge. Sew buttons to Body, 12" (30.5 cm) from top edge and centered with each Strap.

Design by Melissa Leapman.

BUBBLE HAT

 EASY

SIZE INFORMATION
Sizes:
   0-3 months {6 months-12 months}
Fits Head Circumference:
   12{14-16}"/30.5{35.5-40.5} cm

Size Note: We have printed the instructions for the sizes in different colors to make it easier for you to find:
• Size 0-3 months in Blue
• Size 6 months in Pink
• Size 12 months in Green
Instructions in Black apply to all sizes.

GAUGE INFORMATION
In pattern,
   14 sts = 4" (10 cm);
   12 rnds = 2¾" (7 cm)
Gauge Swatch: 4"w x 2¾"h
   (10 cm x 7 cm)
Ch 15.
Row 1: Sc in second ch from hook and in each ch across: 14 sc.
Row 2 (Right side): Ch 1, turn; sc in each sc across.
Row 3: Ch 1, turn; sc in first 2 sc, (work Cluster in next sc, sc in next sc) across: 8 sc and 6 Clusters.
Row 4: Ch 1, turn; sc in each sc and in each Cluster across: 14 sc.
Rows 5 and 6: Ch 1, turn; sc in each sc across.
Rows 7 and 8: Repeat Rows 3 and 4: 14 sc.
Finish off.

STITCH GUIDE
SINGLE CROCHET 2 TOGETHER
   (abbreviated sc2tog)
Pull up a loop in each of next 2 sc, YO and draw through all 3 loops on hook **(counts as one sc)**.

BACK POST DOUBLE CROCHET
   (abbreviated BPdc)
YO, insert hook from **back** to **front** around post of st indicated *(Fig. 10, page 141)*, YO and pull up a loop (3 loops on hook), (YO and draw through 2 loops on hook) twice.

CLUSTER (uses one sc)
★ YO, insert hook in sc indicated, YO and pull up a loop, YO and draw through 2 loops on hook; repeat from ★ 3 times more, YO and draw through all 5 loops on hook, ch 1 to close.

SHOPPING LIST

Yarn (Light Weight) [3]
[3.5 ounces, 340 yards (100 grams, 310 meters) per skein]:
☐ 1 skein

Crochet Hook
☐ Size H (5 mm)
   or size needed for gauge

Additional Supplies
☐ Tapestry needle

RIBBING

Rnd 1 (Right side): Ch 3, YO, insert hook in third ch from hook **(2 skipped chs count as first fdc)**, YO and pull up a loop, YO and draw through one loop on hook **(ch made)**, (YO and draw through 2 loops on hook) twice **(fdc made)**, work 38{42-46} fdc *(Fig. 2, page 139)*; join with slip st to first fdc: 40{44-48} fdc.

Rnd 2: Ch 1, turn; work BPdc around same st as joining, work FPdc around next fdc, ★ work BPdc around next fdc, work FPdc around next fdc; repeat from ★ around; join with slip st to first BPdc.

Rnd 3: Ch 1, turn; work FPdc around same st as joining, work BPdc around next FPdc, ★ work FPdc around next BPdc, work BPdc around next FPdc; repeat from ★ around; join with slip st to first FPdc, do **not** finish off.

BODY

Rnds 1 and 2: Ch 1, turn; sc in each st around; join with slip st to first sc.

Rnd 3: Ch 1, turn; sc in same st as joining, work Cluster in next sc, (sc in next sc, work Cluster in next sc) around; join with slip st to first sc: 20{22-24} sc and 20{22-24} Clusters.

Rnd 4: Ch 1, turn; sc in each sc and in each Cluster around; join with slip st to first sc: 40{44-48} sc.

Rnds 5 and 6: Ch 1, turn; sc in each sc around; join with slip st to first sc.

Rnds 7-10: Repeat Rnds 3-6; at end of Rnd 10, do **not** finish off.

SIZE 0-3 MONTHS ONLY

Rnds 11 and 12: Repeat Rnds 3 and 4: 40 sc.

Rnd 13: Ch 1, turn; sc in same st as joining and in next 2 sc, sc2tog, (sc in next 3 sc, sc2tog) around; join with slip st to first sc: 32 sc.

Rnd 14: Ch 1, turn; sc in each sc around; join with slip st to first sc.

Rnds 15 and 16: Repeat Rnds 3 and 4: 32 sc.

Rnd 17: Ch 1, turn; sc in same st as joining and in next sc, sc2tog, (sc in next 2 sc, sc2tog) around; join with slip st to first sc: 24 sc.

Rnd 18: Ch 1, turn; sc in same st as joining, sc2tog, (sc in next sc, sc2tog) around; join with slip st to first sc: 16 sc.

Rnds 19 and 20: Ch 1, turn; beginning in same st as joining, sc2tog around; join with slip st to first sc: 4 sc.

Finish off, leaving long end for sewing.

SIZE 6 MONTHS ONLY

Rnds 11-16: Repeat Rnds 3-6 once, then repeat Rnds 3 and 4 once **more**: 44 sc.

Rnd 17: Ch 1, turn; sc in same st as joining and in next 2 sc, sc2tog, (sc in next 3 sc, sc2tog) around to last 4 sc, sc in last 4 sc; join with slip st to first sc: 36 sc.

Rnd 18: Ch 1, turn; sc in same st as joining and in next sc, sc2tog, (sc in next 2 sc, sc2tog) around to last 4 sc, sc in last 4 sc; join with slip st to first sc: 28 sc.

Rnds 19 and 20: Repeat Rnds 3 and 4: 28 sc.

Rnd 21: Ch 1, turn, sc in same st as joining, sc2tog, (sc in next st, sc2tog) around to last sc, sc in last sc; join with slip st to first sc: 19 sc.

Rnd 22: Ch 1, turn; beginning in same st as joining, sc2tog around to last sc, sc in last sc; join with slip st to first sc: 10 sc.

Rnd 23: Ch 1, turn; beginning in same st as joining, sc2tog around; join with slip st to first sc, finish off leaving long end for sewing: 5 sc.

BUBBLE HAT

SIZE 12 MONTHS ONLY

Rnds 11-16: Repeat Rnds 3-6 once, then repeat Rnds 3 and 4 once **more**: 48 sc.

Rnd 17: Ch 1, turn; beginning in same st as joining, sc2tog, sc in next 2 sc, (sc2tog, sc in next 3 sc) around to last 4 sc, sc2tog, sc in last 2 sc; join with slip st to first sc: 38 sc.

Rnd 18: Ch 1, turn; sc in same st as joining and in each sc around; join with slip st to first sc.

Rnds 19 and 20: Repeat Rnds 3 and 4: 38 sc.

Rnd 21: Ch 1, turn; (sc in next 2 sc, sc2tog) around to last 6 sc, (sc in next sc, sc2tog) twice; join with slip st to first sc: 28 sc.

Rnd 22: Ch 1, turn; beginning in same st as joining, sc2tog, sc in next 2 sc, sc2tog, ★ sc in next sc, sc2tog, sc in next 2 sc, sc2tog; repeat from ★ around to last sc, sc in last sc; join with slip st to first sc: 20 sc.

Rnds 23 and 24: Repeat Rnds 3 and 4: 20 sc.

Rnd 25: Ch 1, turn; beginning in same st as joining, (sc2tog, sc in next sc, sc2tog, sc in next 2 sc) twice, (sc2tog, sc in next sc) twice; join with slip st to first sc: 14 sc.

Rnd 26: Ch 1, turn; beginning in same st as joining, (sc2tog, sc in next sc) around to last 2 sc, sc in last 2 sc; join with slip st to first sc: 10 sc.

Rnd 27: Ch 1, turn; beginning in same st as joining, sc2tog around; join with slip st to first sc, finish off leaving long end for sewing: 5 sc.

ALL SIZES

Thread tapestry needle with long end and weave needle through sts on last rnd (*Fig. 15, page 142*); pull tightly to close and secure end.

POM-POM

Make one 2" (5 cm) pom-pom (*Figs.16a-c, page 143*); then sew to top of Hat.

Design by Sharon H. Silverman.

0-3 Months

6 Months

12 Months

BOBBLING AWAY BLANKET

 EASY

Finished Size: 33" x 47¾" (84 cm x 121.5 cm)

GAUGE INFORMATION
In pattern, one repeat (25 sts from point-to-point) = 4⅛" (10.5 cm); 16 rows = 4¾" (12 cm)
Gauge Swatch: 8¼"w x 3"h (21 cm x 7.5 cm)
With White, ch 48.
Work same as Body Rows 1-10: 50 sc.
Finish off; cut Lt Blue and Peach.

STITCH GUIDE
BOBBLE (uses one st or sp)
★ YO, insert hook in st or sp indicated, YO and pull up a loop, YO and draw through 2 loops on hook; repeat from ★ 4 times more, YO and draw through all 6 loops on hook.

BODY
With White, ch 192.

Row 1 (Right side): Sc in second ch from hook and in next 10 chs, 3 sc in next ch, sc in next 11 chs, ★ skip next ch, sc in next 11 chs, 3 sc in next ch, sc in next 11 chs; repeat from ★ across changing to Lt Blue in last sc *(Fig. 7b, page 140)*; do **not** cut White: 200 sc.

At the end of each row, do **not** cut previous color unless specified. Unused colors are carried loosely along the sides and are crocheted over when working the Edging.

Row 2: Ch 1, turn; skip first sc, sc in next sc, (ch 1, skip next sc, sc in next sc) 5 times, 3 sc in next sc, sc in next sc, ★ (ch 1, skip next sc, sc in next sc) 5 times, skip next 2 sc, sc in next sc, (ch 1, skip next sc, sc in next sc) 5 times, 3 sc in next sc, sc in next sc; repeat from ★ across to last 11 sc, (ch 1, skip next sc, sc in next sc) 4 times, ch 1, skip next 2 sc, sc in last sc changing to Peach: 120 sc and 80 ch-1 sps.

Row 3: Ch 1, turn; skip first sc, (sc in next ch-1 sp, ch 1) 5 times, skip next sc, sc in next sc, 3 sc in next sc, sc in next sc, ★ (ch 1, sc in next ch-1 sp) 5 times, skip next 2 sc, (sc in next ch-1 sp, ch 1) 5 times, skip next sc, sc in next sc, 3 sc in next sc, sc in next sc; repeat from ★ across to last 5 ch-1 sps, (ch 1, sc in next ch-1 sp) 4 times, ch 1, skip next ch-1 sp, sc in last sc changing to White.

SHOPPING LIST

Yarn
(Light Weight) [3]
[3.5 ounces, 340 yards (100 grams, 310 meters) per skein]:
☐ 1 skein

Crochet Hook
☐ Size H (5 mm)
or size needed for gauge

Additional Supplies
☐ Tapestry needle

Continue working in the following stripe sequence: One row each, ★ White, Lt Blue, Peach; repeat from ★ for sequence.

Rows 4-8: Ch 1, turn; skip first sc, (sc in next ch-1 sp, ch 1) 5 times, skip next sc, sc in next sc, 3 sc in next sc, sc in next sc, ★ (ch 1, sc in next ch-1 sp) 5 times, skip next 2 sc, (sc in next ch-1 sp, ch 1) 5 times, skip next sc, sc in next sc, 3 sc in next sc, sc in next sc; repeat from ★ across to last 5 ch-1 sps, (ch 1, sc in next ch-1 sp) 4 times, ch 1, skip next ch-1 sp, sc in last sc changing to next color.

Row 9: Ch 1, turn; skip first sc, ★ † sc in next ch-1 sp and in next sc, work Bobble in next ch-1 sp, sc in next sc and in next ch-1 sp, work Bobble in next sc, sc in next ch-1 sp and in next sc, work Bobble in next ch-1 sp, sc in next 2 sc, (sc, work Bobble, sc) in next sc, sc in next 2 sc, work Bobble in next ch-1 sp, sc in next sc and in next ch-1 sp, work Bobble in next sc, sc in next ch-1 sp and in next sc, work Bobble in next ch-1 sp †, sc in next sc and in next ch-1 sp, skip next 2 sc; repeat from ★ 6 times more, then repeat from † to † once, sc in next sc, skip next ch-1 sp, sc in last sc changing to next color: 200 sts (144 sc and 56 Bobbles).

Row 10: Ch 1, turn; skip first sc, sc in next 11 sts, 3 sc in next Bobble, ★ sc in next 11 sts, skip next 2 sc, sc in next 11 sts, 3 sc in next Bobble; repeat from ★ across to last 12 sts, sc in next 10 sts, skip next sc, sc in last sc changing to next color.

Row 11: Ch 1, turn; skip first sc, sc in next sc, (ch 1, skip next sc, sc in next sc) 5 times, 3 sc in next sc, sc in next sc, ★ (ch 1, sc in next sc) 5 times, skip next 2 sc, sc in next sc, (ch 1, skip next sc, sc in next sc) 5 times, 3 sc in next sc, sc in next sc; repeat from ★ across to last 11 sc, (ch 1, skip next sc, sc in next sc) 4 times, ch 1, skip next 2 sc, sc in last sc changing to next color: 120 sc and 80 ch-1 sps.

Rows 12-147: Repeat Rows 4-11, 17 times: 120 sc and 80 ch-1 sps.

Rows 148-154: Ch 1, turn; skip first sc, (sc in next ch-1 sp, ch 1) 5 times, skip next sc, sc in next sc, 3 sc in next sc, sc in next sc, ★ (ch 1, sc in next ch-1 sp) 5 times, skip next 2 sc, (sc in next ch-1 sp, ch 1) 5 times, skip next sc, sc in next sc, 3 sc in next sc, sc in next sc; repeat from ★ across to last 5 ch-1 sps, (ch 1, sc in next ch-1 sp) 4 times, ch 1, skip next ch-1 sp, sc in last sc changing to next color: 200 sts (120 sc and 80 ch-1 sps).

Cut White and Peach ONLY.

Edging
With Lt Blue, ch 1, turn; skip first sc, ★ † sc in next ch-1 sp, (sc in next sc and in next ch-1 sp) 4 times, sc in next 2 sc, 3 sc in next sc, sc in next 2 sc and in next ch-1 sp, (sc in next sc and in next ch-1 sp) 4 times †, skip next 2 sc; repeat from ★ 6 times **more**, then repeat from † to † once, 3 sc in last sc; sc in end of each row across; working in free loops of beginning ch *(Fig. 6b, page 140)*, 3 sc in first ch, sc in next 10 chs, [skip next ch, sc in next 11 chs, 3 sc in next ch, sc in next 11 chs] 7 times, skip next ch, sc in next 10 chs, 3 sc in next ch; sc in end of each row across; 3 sc in first sc on Row 154; join with slip st to first sc, finish off.

Design by Becky Stevens.

BLUE BLOCKS BLANKET

 EASY

Finished Size: 34" x 49" (86.5 cm x 124.5 cm)

GAUGE INFORMATION
17 sts = 4" (10 cm)
Each Square = 7½" (19 cm)
Gauge Swatch: 2¾" (7 cm) square
Work same as Square through Rnd 3: 36 dc and 12 ch-1 sps.

STITCH GUIDE
FRONT POST DOUBLE TREBLE CROCHET (abbreviated FPdtr)
YO 3 times, insert hook from **front** to **back** around post of st indicated *(Fig. 10, page 141)*, YO and pull up a loop (5 loops on hook), (YO and draw through 2 loops on hook) 4 times.

SQUARE (Make 24)
With Blue, ch 4; join with slip st to form a ring.

Rnd 1 (Right side): Ch 3 (**counts as first dc, now and throughout**), 2 dc in ring, ch 1, (3 dc in ring, ch 1) 3 times; join with slip st to first dc, finish off: 12 dc and 4 ch-1 sps.

Note: Loop a short piece of yarn around any stitch to mark Rnd 1 as **right** side.

Rnd 2: With **right** side facing, join White with dc in any ch-1 sp *(see Joining With Dc, page 139)*; (2 dc, ch 1, 3 dc) in same sp, skip next 3 dc, ★ (3 dc, ch 1, 3 dc) in next ch-1 sp, skip next 3 dc; repeat from ★ 2 times **more**; join with slip st to first dc, finish off: 24 dc and 4 ch-1 sps.

SHOPPING LIST

Yarn
(Medium Weight) 4
[5 ounces, 256 yards (141 grams, 234 meters) per skein]:
☐ Lt Blue - 4 skeins
☐ Blue - 4 skeins
☐ White - 2 skeins

Crochet Hook
☐ Size F (3.75 mm)
or size needed for gauge

Additional Supplies
☐ Yarn needle

BLUE BLOCKS BLANKET

Rnd 3: With **right** side facing, join Lt Blue with dc in any ch-1 sp; ch 1, 3 dc in same sp, ch 1, skip next 3 dc, 3 dc in sp **before** next dc *(Fig. 8, page 141)*, ch 1, skip next 3 dc, ★ (3 dc, ch 1) twice in next ch-1 sp, skip next 3 dc, 3 dc in sp **before** next dc, ch 1, skip next 3 dc; repeat from ★ 2 times **more**, 2 dc in same sp as first dc; join with slip st to first dc, do **not** finish off: 36 dc and 12 ch-1 sps.

Rnd 4: Slip st in next corner ch-1 sp, ch 3, (2 dc, ch 1, 3 dc) in same sp, ch 1, (3 dc in next ch-1 sp, ch 1) twice, ★ (3 dc, ch 1) twice in next corner ch-1 sp, (3 dc in next ch-1 sp, ch 1) twice; repeat from ★ 2 times **more**; join with slip st to first dc, finish off: 48 dc and 16 ch-1 sps.

Rnd 5: With **right** side facing, join Blue with dc in any corner ch-1 sp; (2 dc, ch 1, 3 dc) in same sp, ch 1, (3 dc in next ch-1 sp, ch 1) 3 times, ★ (3 dc, ch 1) twice in next corner ch-1 sp, (3 dc in next ch-1 sp, ch 1) 3 times; repeat from ★ 2 times **more**; join with slip st to first dc, finish off: 60 dc and 20 ch-1 sps.

Rnd 6: With **right** side facing, join Lt Blue with dc in any corner ch-1 sp; (2 dc, ch 1, 3 dc) in same sp, ch 1, ★ † 3 dc in next ch-1 sp, skip next dc, dc in next dc, [work FPdtr around first dc of 3-dc group one rnd below next ch-1 sp, dc in ch-1 sp, skip next dc one rnd below, work FPdtr around next dc, skip next dc, dc in next dc] twice, 3 dc in next ch-1 sp, ch 1 †, (3 dc, ch 1) twice in next corner ch-1 sp; repeat from ★ 2 times **more**, then repeat from † to † once; join with slip st to first dc, finish off: 84 sts and 12 ch-1 sps.

Rnd 7: With **right** side facing, join White with dc in any corner ch-1 sp; (2 dc, ch 1, 3 dc) in same sp, ch 1, ★ † 3 dc in next ch-1 sp, ch 1, [skip next 3 sts, 3 dc in next ch-1 sp, ch 1] 3 times, 3 dc in next ch-1 sp, ch 1 †, (3 dc, ch 1) twice in next corner ch-1 sp; repeat from ★ 2 times **more**, then repeat from † to † once; join with slip st to first dc, finish off: 84 dc and 28 ch-1 sps.

BLUE BLOCKS BLANKET

Rnd 8: With **right** side facing, join Blue with dc in any corner ch-1 sp; (2 dc, ch 1, 3 dc) in same sp, ch 1, ★ † 3 dc in next ch-1 sp, ch 1, 3 dc in next ch-1 sp, skip next dc, dc in next dc, [work FPdtr around FPdtr one rnd **below**, dc in next ch-1 sp, work FPdtr around FPdtr one rnd below, skip next dc, dc in next dc] twice, (3 dc in next ch-1 sp, ch 1) twice †, (3 dc, ch 1) twice in next corner ch-1 sp; repeat from ★ 2 times **more**, then repeat from † to † once; join with slip st to first dc, finish off: 108 sts and 20 ch-1 sps.

Rnd 9: With **right** side facing, join Lt Blue with dc in any corner ch-1 sp; ch 1, 3 dc in same sp, ch 1, ★ † (3 dc in next ch-1 sp, ch 1) twice, (skip next 3 sts, 3 dc in next dc, ch 1) 3 times, (3 dc in next ch-1 sp, ch 1) twice †, (3 dc, ch 1) twice in next corner ch-1 sp; repeat from ★ 2 times **more**, then repeat from † to † once, 2 dc in same sp as first dc; join with slip st to first dc, finish off leaving a long end for sewing: 108 dc and 36 ch-1 sps.

ASSEMBLY

Thread yarn needle with long end. With **wrong** sides together and working through **both** loops on **both** pieces, whipstitch 2 Squares together *(Fig. 13a, page 142)*. Join remaining Squares forming 4 vertical strips of 6 Squares each; then join strips together in same manner.

TRIM
First Side

Row 1: With **right** side facing and working across long edge, join Blue with sc in first corner ch-1 sp *(see Joining With Sc, page 138)*; ★ † sc in next 3 dc, (skip next ch, sc in next 3 dc) twice, (sc in next ch and in next 3 dc, skip next ch, sc in next 3 dc) 3 times †, 2 sc in joining; repeat from ★ 4 times **more**, then repeat from † to † once, sc in next corner ch-1 sp: 192 sc.

Row 2: Ch 1, turn; sc in each st across.

Row 3: Ch 1, turn; (sc, dc) in first sc, ★ skip next sc, (sc, dc) in next sc; repeat from ★ across to last 3 sc, skip next sc, sc in last 2 sc.

Rows 4-8: Repeat Rows 2 and 3 twice, then repeat Row 2 once **more**: 192 sc.

Finish off.

Second Side

Working across opposite long edge, work same as First Side: 192 sc.

First End

Row 1: With **right** side facing and working in end of rows on First Side, join Blue with sc in first row; sc in next 7 rows; sc in sp on next Square, ★ † sc in next 3 dc, (skip next ch, sc in next 3 dc) twice, (sc in next ch and in next 3 dc, skip next ch, sc in next 3 dc) 3 times †, 2 sc in joining; repeat from ★ 2 times **more**, then repeat from † to † once, sc in next sp; sc in end of next 8 rows on Second Side: 144 sc.

Rows 2-8: Work same as First Side: 144 sc.

Finish off.

Second End

Working across opposite short edge, work same as First End: 144 sc.

EDGING

Rnd 1: With **right** side facing and working across Row 8 of either End, join Lt Blue with sc in first sc; sc in same st and in each sc across to last sc of End, 4 sc in last sc; sc in end of next 7 rows, sc in each sc across Side, sc in end of next 7 rows; working across Row 8 of next End, 4 sc in first sc, sc in each sc across to last sc of End, 4 sc in last sc; sc in end of next 7 rows, sc in each sc across Side, sc in end of next 7 rows; 2 sc in same st as first sc; join with slip st to first sc.

Rnd 2: Ch 1, sc in same st as joining and in each sc around; join with slip st to first sc, finish off.

Design by Carol Holding.

BLUEBELLS ENSEMBLE

 EASY

GAUGE INFORMATION
The instructions are worked the same for all sizes. Finished measurement is obtained by using a different size hook as recommended under Shopping List **and** achieving the gauge specified below.

In pattern, 22{20-19} sts = 4" (10 cm) and 13 rows = 4¼{4¾-5}"/ 10.75{12-12.75} cm

Gauge Swatch:
5¼{5¾-6}" w x 4¼{4¾-5}" h
13.25{14.5-15.25} cm x
10.75{12-12.75} cm
Ch 31.
Work Rows 1-13 of Cardigan: 29 sts. Finish off.

STITCH GUIDE
SINGLE CROCHET 2 TOGETHER
(abbreviated sc2tog)
(uses next 2 ch-1 sps)
Pull up a loop in each of next 2 ch-1 sps, YO and draw through all 3 loops on hook (**counts as one sc**).

DOUBLE CROCHET 2 TOGETHER
(abbreviated dc2tog) (uses next 2 sts)
★ YO, insert hook in **next** st, YO and pull up a loop, YO and draw through 2 loops on hook; repeat from ★ once **more**, YO and draw through all 3 loops on hook. (**counts as one dc**).

FRONT POST DOUBLE CROCHET
(abbreviated FPdc)
YO, insert hook from **front** to **back** around post of st indicated (*Fig. 10, page 141*), YO and pull up a loop (3 loops on hook), (YO and draw through 2 loops on hook) twice. Skip st **behind** FPdc.

BACK POST DOUBLE CROCHET
(abbreviated BPdc)
YO, insert hook from **back** to **front** around post of FPdc indicated (*Fig. 10, page 141*), YO and pull up a loop (3 loops on hook), (YO and draw through 2 loops on hook) twice. Skip st in **front** of BPdc.

SHOPPING LIST

Yarn
(Light Weight) MEDIUM 4
[6 ounces, 430 yards
(170 grams, 393 meters)
per skein]:
☐ Variegated - 2{2-2} skeins

Crochet Hook
☐ Size Newborn-3 months - Size E (3.5 mm)
☐ Size 3-6 months - Size F (3.75 mm)
☐ Size 6-12 months - Size G (4 mm)
or size needed for gauge

Additional Supplies
☐ ⅝" (17 mm) Buttons - 5
☐ Yarn needle

FRONT POST CLUSTER
(abbreviated FP Cluster)
YO, insert hook from **front** to **back** around post of st indicated *(Fig. 10, page 141)*, YO and pull up a loop, YO and draw through 2 loops on hook, YO, insert hook from **front** to **back** around post of same st, YO and pull up a loop, YO and draw through 2 loops on hook, YO and draw through all 3 loops on hook. Skip st **behind** FP Cluster.

CARDIGAN

Finished Chest Measurement (Buttoned):
19{21-22}"/48.5{53.5-56} cm
Finished Length:
9½{10½-11}"/24{26.5-28} cm

Body
Ch 103.

Row 1: Dc in fourth ch from hook **(3 skipped chs count as first dc)** and in each ch across: 101 dc.

Row 2 (Right side): Ch 3 **(counts as first dc, now and throughout)**, turn; dc in next 4 dc, ★ work FPdc around next dc, dc in next 2 dc, work FP Cluster around next dc, dc in next 2 dc, work FPdc around next dc, dc in next 5 dc; repeat from ★ across: 77 dc, 16 FPdc, and 8 FP Clusters.

Note: Loop a short piece of yarn around any stitch to mark Row 2 as **right** side.

Row 3: Ch 3, turn; dc in next 4 dc, (work BPdc around next FPdc, dc in next 5 sts) across: 85 dc and 16 BPdc.

Row 4: Ch 3, turn; dc in next dc, work FP Cluster around next dc, dc in next 2 dc, ★ work FPdc around next BPdc, dc in next 5 dc, work FPdc around next BPdc, dc in next 2 dc, work FP Cluster around next dc, dc in next 2 dc; repeat from ★ across: 76 dc, 16 FPdc, and 9 FP Clusters.

Row 5: Ch 3, turn; dc in next 4 sts, (work BPdc around next FPdc, dc in next 5 sts) across: 85 dc and 16 BPdc.

Row 6: Ch 3, turn; dc in next 4 dc, ★ work FPdc around next BPdc, dc in next 2 dc, work FP Cluster around next dc, dc in next 2 dc, work FPdc around next BPdc, dc in next 5 dc; repeat from ★ across: 77 dc, 16 FPdc, and 8 FP Clusters.

Rows 7-17: Repeat Rows 3-6 twice, then repeat Rows 3-5 once **more**; do **not** finish off.

Right Front

Row 1: Ch 3, turn; dc in next 4 dc, work FPdc around next BPdc, dc in next 2 dc, work FP Cluster around next dc, dc in next 2 dc, work FPdc around next BPdc, dc in next 5 dc, work FPdc around next BPdc, dc in next 2 dc, work FP Cluster around next dc, dc in next 2 dc, leave remaining sts unworked: 18 dc, 3 FPdc, and 2 FP Clusters.

Row 2: Ch 3, turn; dc in next 4 sts, (work BPdc around next FPdc, dc in next 5 sts) across: 20 dc and 3 BPdc.

Row 3: Ch 3, turn; dc in next dc, work FP Cluster around next dc, dc in next 2 dc, work FPdc around next BPdc, dc in next 5 dc, work FPdc around next BPdc, dc in next 2 dc, work FP Cluster around next dc, dc in next 2 dc, work FPdc around next BPdc, dc in last 5 dc: 18 dc, 3 FPdc, and 2 FP Clusters.

Row 4: Repeat Row 2.

Row 5: Ch 3, turn; dc in next 4 dc, work FPdc around next BPdc, dc in next 2 dc, work FP Cluster around next dc, dc in next 2 dc, work FPdc around next BPdc, dc in next 5 dc, work FPdc around next BPdc, dc in next 2 dc, work FP Cluster around next dc, dc in last 2 dc: 18 dc, 3 FPdc, and 2 FP Clusters.

Row 6: Ch 3, turn; dc in next 4 sts, (work BPdc around next FPdc, dc in next 5 sts) twice, work BPdc around next FPdc, dc in next dc, leave last 4 sts unworked for Neck: 16 dc and 3 BPdc.

Row 7: Ch 3, turn; dc2tog, dc in next 4 dc, work FPdc around next BPdc, dc in next 2 dc, work FP Cluster around next dc, dc in next 2 dc, work FPdc around next BPdc, dc in last 5 dc: 15 dc, 2 FPdc, and 1 FP Cluster.

Row 8: Ch 3, turn; dc in next 4 dc, work BPdc around next FPdc, dc in next 5 sts, work BPdc around next FPdc, dc in next 4 dc, dc2tog: 15 dc and 2 BPdc.

Row 9: Ch 3, turn; dc2tog, dc in next 2 dc, (work FPdc around next BPdc, dc in next 5 dc) twice: 14 dc and 2 FPdc, finish off.

133

BLUEBELLS ENSEMBLE

Back
Row 1: With **right** side facing, skip next st on Row 17 of Body and join yarn in next st; ch 3, dc in next 4 dc, ★ work FPdc around next BPdc, dc in next 2 dc, work FP Cluster around next dc, dc in next 2 dc, work FPdc around next BPdc, dc in next 5 dc; repeat from ★ 3 times **more**, leave remaining sts unworked: 41 dc, 8 FPdc, and 4 FP Clusters.

Row 2: Ch 3, turn; dc in next 4 dc, (work BPdc around next FPdc, dc in next 5 sts) across: 45 dc and 8 BPdc.

Row 3: Ch 3, turn; dc in next dc, work FP Cluster around next dc, dc in next 2 dc, ★ work FPdc around next BPdc, dc in next 5 dc, work FPdc around next BPdc, dc in next 2 dc, work FP Cluster around next dc, dc in next 2 dc; repeat from ★ across: 40 dc, 8 FPdc, and 5 FP Clusters.

Row 4: Repeat Row 2.

Row 5: Ch 3, turn; dc in next 4 dc, ★ work FPdc around next BPdc, dc in next 2 dc, work FP Cluster around next dc, dc in next 2 dc, work FPdc around next BPdc, dc in next 5 dc; repeat from ★ across: 41 dc, 8 FPdc, and 4 FP Clusters.

Rows 6 and 7: Repeat Rows 2 and 3.

LEFT SHOULDER
Row 1: Ch 3, turn; dc in next 4 sts, (work BPdc around next FPdc, dc in next 5 sts) twice, leave remaining sts unworked: 15 dc and 2 BPdc.

Row 2: Ch 3, turn; dc2tog, dc in next 2 dc, (work FPdc around next BPdc, dc in next 5 dc) twice; finish off: 14 dc and 2 FPdc.

RIGHT SHOULDER
Row 1: With **wrong** side facing, skip next 19 sts on Row 7 of Back and join yarn with slip st in next dc; ch 3, dc in next 4 sts, (work BPdc around next FPdc, dc in next 5 sts) twice: 15 dc and 2 BPdc.

Row 2: Ch 3, turn; dc in next 4 dc, work FPdc around next BPdc, dc in next 5 dc, work FPdc around next BPdc, dc in next 3 dc, dc2tog; finish off: 14 dc and 2 FPdc.

Left Front
Row 1: With **right** side facing, skip next st on Row 17 of Body and join yarn with slip st in next st; ch 3, dc in next dc, work FP Cluster around next dc, dc in next 2 dc, work FPdc around next BPdc, dc in next 5 dc, work FPdc around next BPdc, dc in next 2 dc, work FP Cluster around next dc, dc in next 2 dc, work FPdc around next BPdc, dc in last 5 dc: 18 dc, 3 FPdc, and 2 FP Clusters.

Row 2: Ch 3, turn; dc in next 4 sts, (work BPdc around next FPdc, dc in next 5 sts) across: 20 dc and 3 BPdc.

Row 3: Ch 3, turn; dc in next 4 dc, work FPdc around next BPdc, dc in next 2 dc, work FP Cluster around next dc, dc in next 2 dc, work FPdc around next BPdc, dc in next 5 dc, work FPdc around next BPdc, dc in next 2 dc, work FP Cluster around next dc, dc in last 2 dc: 18 dc, 3 FPdc, and 2 FP Clusters.

Row 4: Repeat Row 2.

Row 5: Ch 3, turn; dc in next dc, work FP Cluster around next dc, dc in next 2 dc, work FPdc around next BPdc, dc in next 5 dc, work FPdc around next BPdc, dc in next 2 dc, work FP Cluster around next dc, dc in next 2 dc, work FPdc around next BPdc, dc in last 5 dc: 18 dc, 3 FPdc, and 2 FP Clusters.

Row 6: Turn; slip st in first 5 dc, ch 3, (work BPdc around next FPdc, dc in next 5 sts) across: 16 dc and 3 BPdc.

Row 7: Ch 3, turn; dc in next 4 dc, work FPdc around next BPdc, dc in next 2 dc, work FP Cluster around next dc, dc in next 2 dc, work FPdc around next BPdc, dc in next 5 dc, dc2tog: 15 dc, 2 FPdc, and 1 FP Cluster.

Row 8: Ch 3, turn; dc2tog, dc in next 3 dc, (work BPdc around next FPdc, dc in next 5 sts) twice: 15 dc and 2 BPdc.

Row 9: Ch 3, turn; dc in next 4 dc, work FPdc around next BPdc, dc in next 5 dc, work FPdc around next BPdc, dc in next 3 dc, dc2tog; finish off: 14 dc and 2 FPdc.

Sew shoulder seams.

Sleeve (Make 2)

Beginning at wrist, ch 30; being careful **not** to twist ch, join with slip st in first ch to form a ring.

Rnd 1 (Right side): Ch 1, sc in back ridge of each ch around (*Fig. 4, page 140*); join with slip st to first sc: 30 sc.

Note: Loop a short piece of yarn around any stitch to mark Rnd 1 as **right** side.

Rnds 2 and 3: Ch 1, sc in each sc around; join with slip st to first sc.

Rnd 4: Ch 3, turn; dc in next sc and in each sc around; join with slip st to first dc: 30 dc.

Rnd 5: Ch 3, turn; dc in next dc, work FP Cluster around next dc, dc in next 2 dc, work FPdc around next dc, ★ dc in next 2 dc, work FP Cluster around next dc, dc in next 2 dc, work FPdc around next dc; repeat from ★ around; join with slip st to first dc: 20 dc, 5 FPdc, and 5 FP Clusters.

Rnd 6: Ch 3, turn; work BPdc around next FPdc, ★ dc in next 5 sts, work BPdc around next FPdc; repeat from ★ around to last 4 sts, dc in last 4 sts; join with slip st to first dc: 25 dc and 5 BPdc.

Rnd 7: Ch 3, turn; dc in next 4 dc, ★ work FPdc around next BPdc, dc in next 5 dc; repeat from ★ around; join with slip st to first dc: 25 dc and 5 FPdc.

Rnd 8: Repeat Rnd 6.

Rnd 9: Ch 3, turn; dc in next dc, work FP Cluster around next dc, dc in next 2 dc, work FPdc around next BPdc, ★ dc in next 2 dc, work FP Cluster around next dc, dc in next 2 dc, work FPdc around next BPdc; repeat from ★ around; join with slip st to first dc: 20 dc, 5 FPdc, and 5 FP Clusters.

Rnd 10: Ch 3, turn; work BPdc around next FPdc, 2 dc in next dc, dc in next 3 sts, ★ 2 dc in next dc, work BPdc around next FPdc, 2 dc in next dc, dc in next 3 sts; repeat from ★ around, dc in same st as first dc; join with slip st to first dc: 35 dc and 5 BPdc.

Rnd 11: Ch 3, turn; dc in next 5 dc, work FPdc around next BPdc, ★ dc in next 7 dc, work FPdc around last BPdc; repeat from ★ around; join with slip st to first dc: 35 dc and 5 FPdc.

Rnd 12: Ch 3, turn; work BPdc around next FPdc, ★ dc in next 7 sts, work BPdc around next FPdc; repeat from ★ around to last 6 sts, dc in last 6 sts; join with slip st to first dc: 35 dc and 5 BPdc.

Rnd 13: Ch 3, turn; dc in next dc, work FP Cluster around next dc, dc in next 3 dc, work FPdc around next BPdc, ★ dc in next 3 dc, work FP Cluster around next dc, dc in next 3 dc, work FPdc around next BPdc; repeat from ★ around to last dc, dc in last dc; join with slip st to first dc: 30 dc, 5 FPdc, and 5 FP Clusters.

Rnd 14: Repeat Rnd 12.

Rnds 15-17: Repeat Rnds 11-13.

Finish off leaving a long end for sewing.

Sew Sleeves into armhole, matching turning ch of Sleeve to skipped st at base of armhole.

Edging

Rnd 1: With **right** side facing and working in free loops of beginning ch (*Fig. 6b, page 140*), join yarn with sc in first ch on lower left edge of Body (*see Joining With Sc, page 138*), 2 sc in same st, sc in next 99 chs, 3 sc in next ch; working across Right Front, 2 sc in end of each row across to corner of neck edge, 3 sc in corner dc, sc evenly around neck edge to next corner, 3 sc in corner dc; working across Left Front, 2 sc in end of each row across; join with slip st to first sc.

Rnd 2: Slip st in next sc, ch 1, 3 sc in same st, ★ sc in each sc across to next corner sc, 3 sc in next corner sc; repeat from ★ 2 times **more**, sc in each sc around; join with slip st to first sc.

Boy's Rnd 3 (Buttonhole Rnd): Slip st in next sc, ch 1, 3 sc in same st, (sc in each sc across to corner sc, 3 sc in corner sc) 3 times, sc in next sc, ch 3, skip next 3 sc (buttonhole), ★ sc in next 7 sc, ch 3, skip next 3 sc; repeat from ★ 3 times **more**, sc in last 4 sc; join with slip st to first sc.

BLUEBELLS ENSEMBLE

Girl's Rnd 3 (Buttonhole Rnd): Slip st in next sc, ch 1, 3 sc in same st, sc in each sc across to next corner sc, 3 sc in corner sc, sc in next 4 sc, ch 3, skip next 3 sc (buttonhole), ★ sc in next 7 sc, ch 3, skip next 3 sc; repeat from ★ 3 times **more**, sc in next sc, 3 sc in corner sc, sc in each sc across to next corner sc, 3 sc in corner sc, sc in each sc around; join with slip st to first sc.

Boy's and Girl's - Rnd 4: Ch 1, sc in each sc and in each ch around, working 3 sc in each corner sc; join with slip st to first sc.

Rnd 5: Ch 1, sc in each sc around, working 3 sc in each corner sc; join with slip st to first sc, finish off.

Sew buttons to front, opposite buttonholes.

CAP

Starting at bottom edge of Cap, ch 60, being careful not to twist ch, join with slip st to form a ring.

Rnd 1: Ch 3 (**counts as first dc, now and throughout**), turn; dc in back ridge of each ch around (**Fig. 4, page 140**); join with slip st to first dc: 60 dc.

Rnd 2: Ch 3, dc in next dc, work FP Cluster around next dc, dc in next 2 dc, work FPdc around next dc, ★ dc in next 2 dc, work FP Cluster around next dc, dc in next 2 dc, work FPdc around next dc; repeat from ★ around; join with slip st to first dc: 40 dc, 10 FPdc, and 10 FP Clusters.

Rnds 3 and 4: Ch 3, dc in next dc, work FP Cluster around next FP Cluster, dc in next 2 dc, work FPdc around next FPdc, ★ dc in next 2 dc, work FP Cluster around next FP Cluster, dc in next 2 dc, work FPdc around next FPdc; repeat from ★ around; join with slip st to first dc.

Rnd 5 (Increase rnd): Ch 3, 2 dc in next dc, work FP Cluster around next FP Cluster, 2 dc in next dc, dc in next dc, work FPdc around next FPdc, ★ dc in next dc, 2 dc in next dc, work FP Cluster around next FP Cluster, 2 dc in next dc, dc in next dc, work FPdc around next FPdc; repeat from ★ around; join with slip st to first dc: 60 dc, 10 FPdc, and 10 FP Clusters.

Rnd 6: Ch 3, dc in Back Loop Only of each st around (**Fig. 5, page 140**); join with slip st to first dc: 80 dc.

Rnd 7: Ch 3, dc2tog, work FP Cluster around next dc, dc2tog, dc in next dc, work FPdc around next dc, ★ dc in next dc, dc2tog, work FP Cluster around next dc, dc2tog, dc in next dc, work FPdc around next dc; repeat from ★ around; join with slip st to first dc: 40 dc, 10 FPdc, and 10 FP Clusters.

Rnd 8: Ch 2, dc in next dc, work FP Cluster around next FP Cluster, dc2tog, work FPdc around next FPdc, ★ dc2tog, work FP Cluster around next FP Cluster, dc2tog, work FPdc around next FPdc; repeat from ★ around; skip beginning ch 2 and join with slip st to top of first dc: 20 dc, 10 FPdc, and 10 FP Clusters.

Rnd 9: Ch 3, work FP Cluster around next FP Cluster, dc in next dc, work FPdc around next FPdc, ★ dc in next dc, work FP Cluster around next FP Cluster, dc in next dc, work FPdc around next FPdc; repeat from ★ around; join with slip st to first dc.

Rnd 10: Ch 3, work FP Cluster around next FP Cluster, ★ dc in next dc, dc2tog, work FP Cluster around next FP Cluster; repeat from ★ around to last 2 sts, dc2tog; join with slip st to first dc: 20 dc and 10 FP Clusters.

Rnd 11: Ch 2, FP Cluster around next FP Cluster, ★ dc2tog, FP Cluster around next FP Cluster; repeat from ★ around to last dc, dc in last dc; skip beginning ch 2 and join with slip st to first FP Cluster: 10 dc and 10 FP Clusters.

Rnd 12: Ch 1, sc2tog around; join with slip st to first sc, finish off leaving a long end for sewing: 10 sc.

With yarn needle, weave end through remaining 10 sc and draw up tightly. Secure yarn on wrong side of work.

Brim

With joining at center back, place marker at Center Front beneath a FP Cluster. Count 12 sts on each side of Center Front Cluster and place marker beneath a FP Cluster.

Row 1: With **wrong** side facing, holding two strands of yarn together, and working in Back Loops Only of each ch, join yarn with slip st in first marked ch; sc in next 23 chs, slip st in next marked ch: 2 slip sts and 23 sc.

Row 2: Ch 1, turn; working in Front Loops Only, skip first slip st, sc2tog, hdc in next 3 sc, dc in next 13 sc, hdc in next 3 sc, sc2tog, leave remaining st unworked: 21 sts.

Row 3: Turn; slip st in first sc, working in both loops, sc in next 19 sts, slip st in last st; finish off.

Edging

With **wrong** side of Cap facing, join single strand of yarn with slip st in same st as last sc of Row 1 of Brim; sc in each ch around to opposite side of Brim, slip st in same st as first sc of Brim; finish off: 35 sc.

POM-POM

Make a 1½" (4 cm) pom-pom *(Figs. 16a-c, page 143)*. Sew securely to top of Cap.

BOOTIES
Sole
Ch 15.

Rnd 1 (Right side): 2 Dc in fourth ch from hook **(3 skipped chs count as first dc)**, dc in next ch and in each ch across to last ch, 5 dc in last ch; working in free loops of beginning ch *(Fig. 6b, page 140)*, dc in next 10 chs, 2 dc in same ch as first dc; join with slip st to first dc: 30 dc.

Note: Loop a short piece of yarn around any stitch to mark Rnd 1 as **right** side.

Rnd 2: Ch 3 **(counts as first dc, now and throughout)**, 2 dc in each of next 2 dc, hdc in next 3 dc, sc in next 3 dc, hdc in next 3 dc, dc in next dc, 2 dc in each of next 5 dc, dc in next dc, hdc in next 3 dc, sc in next 3 dc, hdc in next 3 dc, 2 dc in each of next 2 dc; join with slip st to first dc, do **not** finish off: 39 sts.

Sides

Rnd 1: Ch 3, dc in Back Loop Only of next st and each st around *(Fig. 5, page 140)*; join with slip st to both loops of first dc: 39 dc.

Rnd 2: Ch 3, working in both loops, dc in next dc, work FP Cluster around next dc, ★ dc in next 2 dc, work FP Cluster around next dc; repeat from ★ around; join with slip st to first dc: 26 dc and 13 FP Clusters.

Rnd 3: Ch 3, dc in next dc, work FP Cluster around next FP Cluster, (dc in next 2 dc, work FP Cluster around next FP Cluster) 3 times, (dc2tog, work FP Cluster around next FP Cluster) 5 times, (dc in next 2 dc, work FP Cluster around next FP Cluster) 4 times; join with slip st to first dc: 21 dc and 13 FP Clusters.

Rnd 4: Ch 1, sc in first 11 sts, hdc in next st, dc2tog 5 times, hdc in next st, sc in last 11 sts; join with slip st to first sc: 29 sts.

Cuff

Rnd 1 (Eyelet rnd): Ch 3 **(counts as first hdc plus ch 1)**, skip next st, (hdc in next st, ch 1, skip next st) 5 times, (dc in next st, ch 1, skip next st) 4 times, (hdc in next st, ch 1, skip next st) 4 times, hdc in next st, ch 1; join with slip st to first hdc: 15 ch-1 sps.

Rnd 2: Ch 1, 2 sc in each ch-1 sp around; join with slip st to first sc: 30 sc.

Rnd 3: Ch 3, dc in next sc and in each sc around; join with slip st to first dc: 30 dc.

Rnd 4: Ch 3, dc in next dc, work FP Cluster around next dc, ★ dc in next 2 dc, work FP Cluster around dc; repeat from ★ around; join with slip st to first dc: 20 dc and 10 FP Clusters.

Rnd 5: Ch 3, dc in next dc, work FP Cluster around next FP Cluster, ★ dc in next 2 dc, work FP Cluster around next FP Cluster; repeat from ★ around; join with slip st to first dc.

Rnd 6: Ch 1, turn; sc in each st around; join with slip st to first sc, finish off: 30 sc.

Tie

Ch 81, slip st in back ridge of second ch from hook and in each ch across; finish off: 80 slip sts.

Beginning at center front of Bootie, weave Tie through Eyelet Rnd.

Design by Mary Ann Sipes.

GENERAL INSTRUCTIONS

ABBREVIATIONS

BP	Back Post
BPdc	Back Post double crochet(s)
ch(s)	chain(s)
cm	centimeters
dc	double crochet(s)
dc2tog	double crochet 2 together
dc3tog	double crochet 3 together
fdc	Foundation double crochet
fsc	Foundation single crochet
FP	Front Post
FPdc	Front Post double crochet(s)
FPdtr	Front Post double treble crochet(s)
FPtr	Front Post treble crochet(s)
hdc	half double crochet(s)
mm	millimeters
Rnd(s)	Round(s)
sc	single crochet(s)
sc2tog	single crochet 2 together
sc3tog	single crochet 3 together
sp(s)	space(s)
st(s)	stitch(es)
tr	treble crochet(s)
YO	yarn over

SYMBOLS & TERMS

★ — work instructions following ★ as many **more** times as indicated in addition to the first time.

† to † — work all instructions from first † to second † as **many** times as specified.

( ) or [ ] — work enclosed instructions **as many** times as specified by the number immediately following **or** work all enclosed instructions in the stitch or space indicated **or** contains explanatory remarks.

colon (:) — the number(s) given after a colon at the end of a row or round denote(s) the number of stitches or spaces you should have on that row or round.

GAUGE

Exact gauge is **essential** for proper size. Before beginning your project, make the sample swatch given in the individual instructions in the yarn and hook specified. After completing the swatch, measure it, counting your stitches and rows/rounds carefully. If your swatch is larger or smaller than specified, **make another, changing hook size to get the correct gauge.** Keep trying until you find the size hook that will give you the specified gauge.

JOINING WITH SC

When instructed to join with a sc, begin with a slip knot on the hook. Insert hook in stitch or space indicated, YO and pull up a loop, YO and draw through both loops on hook.

CROCHET TERMINOLOGY	
UNITED STATES	**INTERNATIONAL**
slip stitch (slip st)	= single crochet (sc)
single crochet (sc)	= double crochet (dc)
half double crochet (hdc)	= half treble crochet (htr)
double crochet (dc)	= treble crochet (tr)
treble crochet (tr)	= double treble crochet (dtr)
double treble crochet (dtr)	= triple treble crochet (ttr)
triple treble crochet (tr tr)	= quadruple treble crochet (qtr)
skip	= miss

■□□□ BASIC	Projects using basic stitches. May include basic increases and decreases.
■■□□ EASY	Projects may include simple stitch patterns, color work, and/or shaping.
■■■□ INTERMEDIATE	Projects may include involved stitch patterns, color work, and/or shaping.
■■■■ COMPLEX	Projects may include complex stitch patterns, color work, and/or shaping using a variety of techniques and stitches simultaneously.

CROCHET HOOKS																
U.S.	B-1	C-2	D-3	E-4	F-5	G-6	7	H-8	I-9	J-10	K-10½	L-11	M/N-13	N/P-15	P/Q	Q	S
Metric - mm	2.25	2.75	3.25	3.5	3.75	4	4.5	5	5.5	6	6.5	8	9	10	15	16	19

JOINING WITH DC

When instructed to join with a dc, begin with a slip knot on the hook. YO, holding loop on hook, insert hook in stitch or space indicated, YO and pull up a loop (3 loops on hook), (YO and draw through 2 loops on hook) twice.

FOUNDATION SINGLE CROCHET (abbreviated fsc)

Ch 2, insert hook in second ch from hook, YO and pull up a loop, YO and draw through one loop on hook (**ch made**), YO and draw through both loops on hook (**first fsc made**), ★ insert hook in ch at base of last fsc made (**Fig. 1**), YO and pull up a loop, YO and draw through one loop on hook (**ch made**), YO and draw through both loops on hook (**fsc made**); repeat from ★ for each additional fsc.

Fig. 1

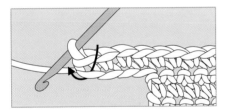

FOUNDATION DOUBLE CROCHET (abbreviated fdc)

Ch 3, YO, insert hook in third ch from hook, YO and pull up a loop, YO and draw through one loop on hook (**ch made**), (YO and draw through 2 loops on hook) twice (**first fdc made**), ★ YO, insert hook in ch at base of last fdc made (**Fig. 2**), YO and pull up a loop, YO and draw through one loop on hook (**ch made**), (YO and draw through 2 loops on hook) twice (**fdc made**); repeat from ★ for each additional fdc.

Fig. 2

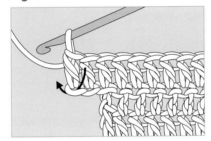

ADJUSTABLE LOOP

Wind the yarn around two fingers to form a ring (**Fig. 3a**), slide the yarn off your fingers and grasp the strands at the top of the ring (**Fig. 3b**). Insert the hook from **front** to **back** into the ring, pull up a loop, YO and draw through the loop on hook to lock the ring (**Fig. 3c**).

Working around **both** strands, work stitches in the ring as specified, then pull the yarn end to close (**Fig. 3d**).

Fig. 3a

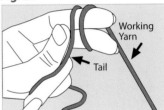

Fig. 3b

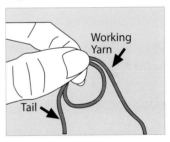

Fig. 3c

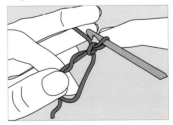

Fig. 3d

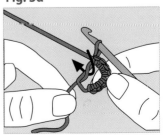

Yarn Weight Symbol & Names	LACE 0	SUPER FINE 1	FINE 2	LIGHT 3	MEDIUM 4	BULKY 5	SUPER BULKY 6	JUMBO 7
Type of Yarns in Category	Fingering, size 10 crochet thread	Sock, Fingering, Baby	Sport, Baby	DK, Light Worsted	Worsted, Afghan, Aran	Chunky, Craft, Rug	Super Bulky, Roving	Jumbo, Roving
Crochet Gauge* Ranges in Single Crochet to 4" (10 cm)	32-42 sts**	21-32 sts	16-20 sts	12-17 sts	11-14 sts	8-11 sts	6-9 sts	5 sts and fewer
Advised Hook Size Range	Steel*** 6 to 8, Regular hook B-1	B-1 to E-4	E-4 to 7	7 to I-9	I-9 to K-10½	K-10½ to M/N-13	M/N-13 to Q	Q and larger

*GUIDELINES ONLY: The chart above reflects the most commonly used gauges and hook sizes for specific yarn categories.

** Lace weight yarns are usually crocheted with larger hooks to create lacy openwork patterns. Accordingly, a gauge range is difficult to determine. Always follow the gauge stated in your pattern.

*** Steel crochet hooks are sized differently from regular hooks–the higher the number, the smaller the hook, which is the reverse of regular hook sizing.

MARKERS

Markers are used to help distinguish the beginning of each round being worked. Place a 2" (5 cm) scrap piece of yarn before the first stitch of each round, moving marker after each round is complete.

BACK RIDGE

Work only in loops indicated by arrows *(Fig. 4)*.

Fig. 4

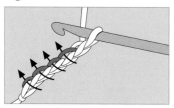

BACK OR FRONT LOOP ONLY

Work only in loop(s) indicated by arrow *(Fig. 5)*.

Fig. 5

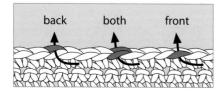

FREE LOOPS OF A CHAIN

After working in Back or Front Loops Only on a row or round, there will be a ridge of unused loops. These are called the free loops. Later, where instructed to work in the free loops of the same row or round, work in these loops *(Fig. 6a)*.

When instructed to work in free loops of a beginning ch, work in loop indicated by arrow *(Fig. 6b)*.

Fig. 6a   **Fig. 6b**

CHANGING COLORS

To change colors while joining with a slip st, drop yarn, insert hook in first st, hook new yarn and draw through st and loop on hook *(Fig. 7a)*.

Fig. 7a

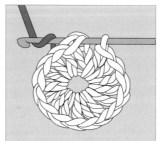

To change colors at the end of or middle of a row, work last st to within one step of completion, drop yarn, with new yarn, YO and draw through remaining 2 loops on hook *(Fig. 7b, 7c, 7d or 7e)*. Do **not** cut old yarn unless instructed.

Fig. 7b

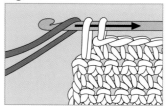

Fig. 7c

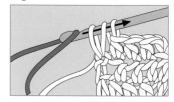

Fig. 7d

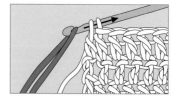

Fig. 7e

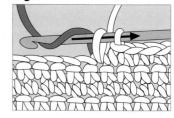

WORKING IN A SPACE BEFORE A STITCH

When instructed to work in a space **before** a stitch or in spaces **between** stitches, insert hook in space indicated by arrow *(Fig. 8)*.

Fig. 8

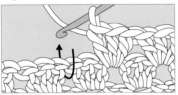

WORKING IN FRONT OF, AROUND, OR BEHIND A STITCH

Work in stitch indicated, inserting hook in direction of arrow *(Fig. 9)*.

Fig. 9

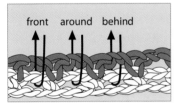

POST STITCH

Work around post of stitch indicated, inserting hook in direction of arrow *(Fig. 10)*.

Fig. 10

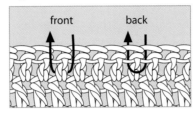

CROSS STITCH
(abbreviated Cross St)

Skip next st, dc in next st, working around dc just made *(Fig. 11a)*, dc in skipped st *(Fig. 11b)*.

Fig. 11a

Fig. 11b

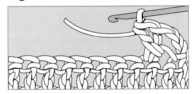

REVERSE SINGLE CROCHET
(abbreviated reverse sc)

Working from **left** to **right**, ★ insert hook in st/row to right of hook *(Fig. 12a)*, YO and draw through, under and to left of loop on hook (2 loops on hook) *(Fig. 12b)*, YO and draw through both loops on hook *(Fig. 12c)* (**reverse sc made**, *Fig. 12d*); repeat from ★ across.

Fig. 12a

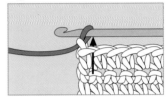

Fig. 12b

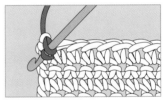

Fig. 12c

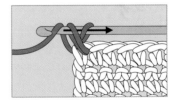

Fig. 12d

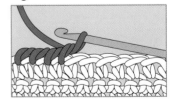

WHIPSTITCH

To whipstitch two pieces together. With **wrong** sides together, sew through both pieces once to secure the beginning of the seam, leaving an ample yarn end to weave in later. Insert the needle from **front** to **back** through **both** loops on **both** pieces *(Fig. 13a)* **or** through **inside** loops only of each stitch on **both** pieces *(Fig. 13b)* **or** in end of rows *(Fig. 13c)*. Bring the needle around and insert it from **front** to **back** through the next loops of **both** pieces. Continue in this manner across to corner, keeping the sewing yarn fairly loose.

Fig. 13a

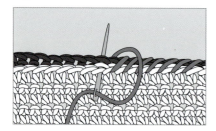

Fig. 13b

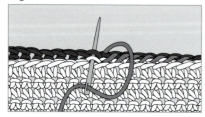

Fig. 13c

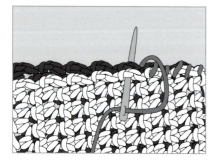

To whipstitch a piece to the Head, insert the needle through the Head or Body, leaving the yarn end inside. Insert the needle from **front** to **back** through both strands on the piece, then through a stitch on the Head or Body *(Fig. 13d)*. Bring the needle around and insert it through the next strands on the piece then through a stitch on the Head or Body. Continue working in same manner.

Fig. 13d

Fig. 13d

MATTRESS STITCH

With the **right** side of both edges facing you and matching stitches, sew through both sides once to secure the beginning of the seam. Insert the needle from **back** to **front** through two strand on one side *(Fig. 14a)*, then from **back** to **front** on the other side *(Fig. 14b)*. Continue in this manner drawing seam together as you work. This will create a flat seam.

Fig. 14a

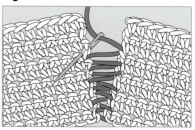

Fig. 14b

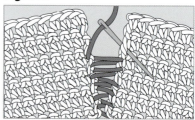

WEAVING THROUGH STITCHES

Thread the yarn needle with the long end and weave it through the stitches on the last round worked *(Fig. 15)*.

Fig. 15

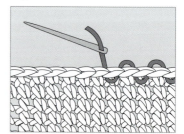

POM-POM

Cut a piece of cardboard 3" (7.5 cm) wide and half as long as instructed in individual instructions.

Wind the yarn around the width of cardboard until it is approximately ½" (12 mm) thick in the middle *(Fig. 16a)*. Carefully slip the yarn off the cardboard and firmly tie an 18" (45.5 cm) length of yarn around the middle *(Fig. 16b)*. Leave yarn ends long enough to attach the pom-pom. Cut the loops on both ends and trim the pom-pom into a smooth ball *(Fig. 16c)*.

Fig. 16a

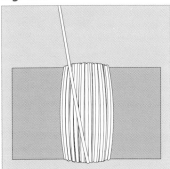

Fig. 16b

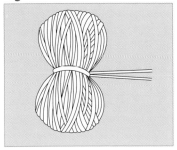

Fig. 16c

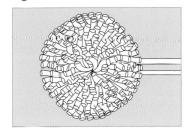

EMBROIDERY STITCHES

Backstitch

The backstitch is worked from right to left. Come up at 1, go down at 2 and come up at 3 *(Fig. 17)*. The second stitch is made by going down at 1 and coming up at 4.

Fig. 17

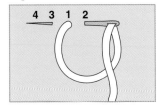

Straight Stitch

Straight stitch is just what the name implies, a single, straight stitch. Come up at 1 and go down at 2 *(Fig. 18)*.

Fig. 18

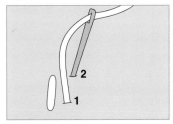

Satin Stitch

Satin stitch is a series of straight stitches worked side by side so they touch but do not overlap *(Fig. 19a)* or come out of and go into the same st *(Fig. 19b)*. Come up at odd numbers and go down at even numbers.

Fig. 19a   **Fig. 19b**

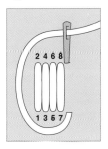 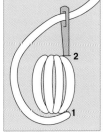

Outline Stitch

Bring needle up at 1, leaving an end to be woven in later. Holding yarn **above** with thumb, insert needle down at 2 and up again at 3 (halfway between 1 and 2) *(Fig. 20a)*; pull through. Insert needle down at 4 and up again at 2, making sure yarn is above needle *(Fig. 20b)*; pull through.

Fig. 20a

Fig. 20b

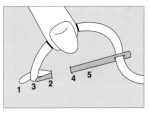

Running Stitch

Running stitch is a series of straight stitches that weave in and out of the fabric. Com up at 1, go down at 2, come up at 3, and go down at 4 *(Fig. 21)*. Continue in same manner.

Fig. 21

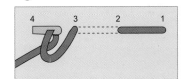

HOW TO FOLD & SEW

What we have is basically origami in yarn with the correct folds creating a sweet little Sweater.

When you have finished the last row of the Neck Shaping of the Basic Sweater, it should look like **Photo A** with a wrong side row just completed and a safety pin on the loop you dropped from your hook. At this point, it's hard to identify the parts of the Sweater, much less imagine where you need to sew the seams.

So let's take a look at **Photo A**. The two corners on the last row are the bottom corners on the fronts of the Sweater, left (1) and right (2). The last stitch with the safety pin is the top of the left front (3). The top of the right front is the first stitch on that same row (4). The beginning chain is at the top of the photo (5) and the last row on the Body is indicated at (6).

With the wrong side still facing, fold the left front so that the last row on the Body (6) meets with the beginning chain (5) as shown in **Photo B**. The right sides of the left front and the back are together. Sew the shoulder/sleeve seam from the last row of the Body across.

Fold the right front in the same fashion and sew the seam as shown in **Photo C**.

Turn the Sweater right side out.

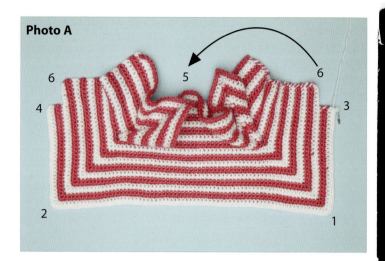

Photo A

Photo B

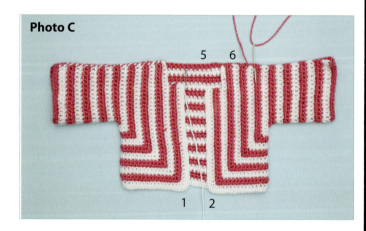

Photo C

We have made every effort to ensure that these instructions are accurate and complete. We cannot, however, be responsible for human error, typographical mistakes, or variations in individual work.

Production Team: Instructional/ Technical Editor - Lois J. Long; Senior Graphic Artist - Lora Puls; Graphic Artist - Maddy Ross; Photo Stylist - Lori Wenger; and Photographer - Jason Masters.

Copyright © 2019 by Leisure Arts, Inc., 104 Champs Blvd., STE 100, Maumelle, AR 72113-6738, www.leisurearts.com. All rights reserved. This publication is protected under federal copyright laws. Reproduction or distribution of this publication or any other Leisure Arts publication, including publications which are out of print, is prohibited unless specifically authorized. This includes, but is not limited to, any form of reproduction or distribution on or through the Internet, including posting, scanning, or e-mail transmission.

Library of Congress Control Number: 2019937365
Made in China